HEALING
RELATIONSHIPS

This book is dedicated to the loving memory of

my Mother,
Oma Moseley,

who taught me the power of words

&

my Daddy,
Fred Moseley,

who taught me how to play with words

HEALING RELATIONSHIPS

A Preaching Model

DAN MOSELEY

CHALICE PRESS

ST. LOUIS, MISSOURI

Cover image: FotoSearch
Cover and interior design: Elizabeth Wright

Visit Chalice Press on the World Wide Web at
www.chalicepress.com

10 9 8 7 6 5 4 3 2 1   09 10 11 12 13 14 15 16

Library of Congress Cataloging-in-Publication Data
Moseley, Dan.
  Healing relationships : a preaching model / by Dan Moseley.
     p. cm.
  ISBN 978-0-8272-1455-2
  1. Preaching. 2. Interpersonal relations--Religious
aspects–Christianity–Sermons. 3. Sermons, American. I. Title.

BV4222.M67 2008
251–dc22

                                                  2008026811

Contents

Prelude

This book is written by a practitioner of preaching for practitioners of preaching. It is, therefore, structured the way practitioners work rather than the way academics work.

Practitioners preach. That is our primary task. Those who preach in congregations center their lives on the relentless return of the Sabbath. Every seven days the preacher must speak a word and hope that within her words people will be able to sort out a Word from the divine. Every seven days the preacher takes a text and seeks to shed a glimmer of light on the life of the community to whom she speaks. After speaking words for a designated period of time, she walks out of the pulpit only to begin reflecting on what she will say in seven more days. Unlike the academic, whose work it is to reflect on the scripture that is the life and work of the preacher and then comment on it, the preacher's life is designed to comment, reflect on life for seven days, and then comment again. The preacher's life is spent in reading and reflecting on the lives of those around him. He spends some time reading and reflecting on scripture and on the thoughts of those who write books and articles, but most of his time is spent reading the life of the community he serves.

On the day designated for community worship, the preacher then is charged with speaking words again. If she has been able to read the texts and read the life of her community well, she might speak in a way that sheds some insight into the life of the listeners. That is the goal.

As this book is by a practitioner for practitioners, it will intersperse reflections on preaching with sermons. My hope is that the net result of the journey through this book will be a sense of how the life we live and reflections we have on that life form and shape the sermons that we preach.

I originally preached the sermons reprinted in this book at the Chautauqua Institution in Chautauqua, New York. These oral presentations were preached over a six-day period in an outdoor amphitheater and therefore flow less like literature and more like a conversation. Chautauqua was established 125 years ago for the purpose of training Methodist Sunday School Teachers and has developed into a summer event for thousands of people. By focusing through the lenses of education, recreation, religion and the arts, it helps people enrich their understanding and their lives.

I have selected these particular sermons because they reflect what I believe about preaching. They are designed to facilitate a relationship between the characters within the sermon and the listeners in the pew.

What I share in this book is not simply the compilation of my mind's reflection. It is the result of preaching for over thirty years to several congregations. I am grateful to the First Christian Church in Roaring Springs, Kentucky; Emerson Park Christian Church in Kansas City, Kansas; First Christian Church in Midwest City, Oklahoma; and The Vine Street Christian Church in Nashville, Tennessee. The members and friends of these congregations listened patiently to me for years and helped me discover what I am sharing in this book.

I am also grateful to the students, faculty, and administration at Christian Theological Seminary in Indianapolis, Indiana. This institution called me to a chair designed to be occupied by a long-term practitioner of the art of ministry. They have nurtured me with gentle and patient presence, with enough distance to allow me to live through pain and see what I could discover in it. They have encouraged me as I have come to a new way of being. My relationship with them has helped me produce this book.

I am also grateful to the Cathedral College in Washington, D.C. for regular invitations to be a part of their faculty. They have allowed me to explore new ideas that were emerging in my life and have created a sacred place for the sharing of these ideas with interested preachers.

I thank Ron Allen, my colleague in preaching at Christian Theological Seminary, for his patient and warm encouraging presence. Ron has believed in me and has created occasions for me to be with other professors of preaching as we reflected on what listeners of preaching have to teach us.

Barbara Brown Taylor has also been an important friend in the shaping of my life as a teacher of preaching. She has offered concise and pointed words of encouragement as we shared our own journeys from the pulpit to the classroom.

I am especially grateful to Callie Smith, a former student at Christian Theological Seminary, for her work on this manuscript. Callie has read and discussed it with me over months of writing and rewriting. Her honest questions and observations have improved this book's chances of being helpful to others.

I am also deeply grateful to my wife, Deborah, for her patient presence and words of encouragement. It is not always easy to live with someone whose tendency is to carry around strange ideas in his head all day. Sometimes she waits while I worked them through; other times she gently pushes through the forest of words to remind me that life is short and that we have a life to live together.

This book is a collaboration of all those who shared my life and helped me come to realize that hope discovered is more life-giving than hope declared, that grace discovered is more healing than grace declared, that truth discovered is more liberating than truth declared. Because of these gifts of learning, I have found that our lives are more shaped by what we discover than by what we hear. I now believe that transformational preaching requires creating space in which people might be in relationships with others and the Other and through these relationships discover hope, grace, and truth. I believe that when they discover these relationships within and around themselves, they will discover the strength to attend to life and change with the faith that opens them to new life.

The Reluctant Pilgrim Sermon

Leaving Home

Exodus 3:1–12

First a personal word of appreciation for Chautauqua: I was introduced to this institution at a time in my life when I was in transition. These past several years have been occasions for growing, learning, and healing. This institution has been a key part of that. I am grateful for all who have been here and have nurtured the structures and the institutions so that we might be here.

I am also grateful for you, who persist in attempting to explain to others what Chautauqua is, especially my friends Dudley and Jim Seal who tried for years to get me here, and for my friends, Ed and Pat Cole, who accompanied me all these years. And I am grateful for my family for coming to join me this week. Thanks to Joan Brown Campbell, a person whom I have admired through the years, for the invitation to be with you.

A word about this week: You can tell from reading the *Chautauquan* that this is a series of sermons on "The Reluctant Pilgrim." There are many of you here today who will not be here the rest of the week. I hope that there is something in one sermon that will nurture and feed you. But if you do return for some or all of them, I hope there will be some other things that might speak to the journey of the soul that we all travel.

This week we will be walking with a few famous saints. This morning a friend asked me if I was nervous. I told her I would have to live in denial to not be nervous before this many people. But I am not as nervous as I would be if I were standing alone. I have brought a few famous friends this week to accompany me. We will talk with Moses later this morning. Later this week, we will visit Mary Magdalene, Jacob, Elijah, Mary, the mother of Jesus, and Jesus himself as we seek to discover what it is to engage a pilgrimage of faith.

I was recently in Kansas City visiting my mother in a nursing home.[1] My siblings and I rented an apartment where we stay when we visit her. I had never been to the apartment. So I got to the apartment late one night and slept. The next morning, as is my custom when I go to a new place, I went out to mark the territory. I have to explore the landscape around my abode.

I walked through the apartment complex, saw all of the cars and walked by the swimming pool: the typical apartment pool, 4' x 8'. I looked at the fake shingles on the walls of the outside. I went out to the boulevard that runs by the complex: four lanes, not much traffic early in the morning before dawn. As I walked down the boulevard, I saw a man about a block away with a white T-shirt on. On the other side of the street, he ducked into some woods. I had not seen the woods. I love wilderness hikes. Excitedly, I thought, "This is going to be fun, an adventure, right here in the suburbs of Kansas City."

I hurried down the boulevard and cut into the woods. It was early dawn dark in the woods. The trail descended into a stream, and I thought again, "Adventure right here in the suburbs." Then I heard a sound. It was a hissing sound. I cleared my eyes, and I pushed some bushes aside to see where the sound was coming from. I looked, and there about thirty yards away, I saw a half-million dollar house with a sprinkler system: "tsh–tsh–tsh." I felt cheated. No wilderness adventure here.

Not being one to give up, I went back to the trail and walked a bit further. I saw what looked like a stump beside the trail. I got a bit closer. In the dim dawn light, it looked like there was something bright-colored on top of the stump. I got a little closer, and there it was: a sewer pipe with a man-hole cover, and on top of it was a white and red and yellow plastic McDonald's cup. It was then I knew that this was not going to be an adventure into the wilderness. This was a suburban park.

When I walked through that trail, I felt like I do in Barnes & Noble, looking for books and spirituality. In the stacks of books, turning down this aisle, this trail, looking for adventure, pulling out books, leafing through the pages, and finding red and yellow plastic cups—looking for bread and finding popcorn—looking for wine and finding soda pop.

The spiritual journey is one that many of us seek, but one that most of us would avoid at all costs. That which is available to define for us the spiritual life of our souls is often inadequate to feed the hunger deep within our souls. It is the soul that longs to be fed. But so much of what we eat does not satisfy.

We long for the grandeur and the terror of the "Holy," and we come away lamenting with Shirley Valentine in that wonderful little movie *Shirley Valentine,* "I live such a little life."[2] Annie Dillard in her classic pilgrimage, *Pilgrim at Tinker Creek,* wonders about our desire for the Holy, our desire for the mystery, when she asks: "Have we rowed out into the thick darkness, or are we all playing pinochle in the bottom of the boat?"[3] We look for a boat, and we look for the sea, and we look for the mystery, and someone gives us a rule book by which to play the cards.

When I despair in Barnes & Noble, and when I go to Amazon.com and see 15,000 entries on spirituality, I decide to go back to my office. I pull out that little stand of mysterious woods called the Bible and I begin to meet my friends. I meet Moses. I ask Moses to tell me about his journey, and you know what? Moses' spiritual journey was not the result of reading books and deciding to become more spiritual.

Here's what happened. Moses was doing what Moses normally did. Moses was living his life just the way you and I live our lives. He was doing what he was paid to do. He was doing that which provided him security. He was tending the sheep that belonged to his father-in-law. Suddenly there was an incredible burning, described in the Bible as the burning of a bush. But my experience is that the geography of our environment is also in the geography of our soul. There was something in Moses that helped him see the burning in the bush because it resonated with his own burning, his own flame, and his own heart.

We do not know what was burning in Moses, and I am one who is reluctant to psychoanalyze anybody else's journey. I do not want anybody trying to explain mine, because to explain my journey is to lose the mystery. But I have thought about it, and in talking with Moses, I have decided that maybe there was something burning inside him. There was a burning, and it would not be consumed.

Moses had a problem. Moses had two passports in life, a passport to slavery and a passport to royalty. He was born Hebrew. He was put into the water. He was rescued by royalty and raised to reign. He had two passports, and I think Moses might have discovered that the fire inside him had burned up the passport to privilege. I think maybe he had lived among his people long enough to realize that that was not his identity. His picture was no longer on the passport.

The passport to privilege was burning, and it burned intensely within him. As it burned, it consumed the cotton in his ears and the scales on his eyes. He could hear his people cry, and he could see their suffering and their pain. That was the burning that caused Moses to leave home. Something caused the insulation around his heart to fall away, and he became one with those who were his brothers and sisters, those who were wounded and those who were oppressed.

When Moses told me his burning, I felt a memory of my own for I, too, have been stripped of the insulation that protected me from common humanity. My wife of thirty-one years died of cancer after struggling with it for three years, and when she died, something in my world collapsed. All the protection that I had built up around me, all of the theology, all of the language, all of the words that protected me from the pain disappeared. The words that I spoke felt hollow within me, and they began to lose their power to define or protect me. They would no longer work. They had been burned in the fire of grief.

It is hard when your house is gone. It is hard when that which protects you disappears. You feel so intensely the pain and the suffering of everyone around you. You hear the cries, and you feel the pull to leave home, because somewhere along the line, it seems as if home left you. You no longer feel at home. So I understand Moses. I understand the fire, and I understand the longing and the yearning to leave home.

It is dangerous and hard to leave home, and most of us do not want to do that. Most of us do not want to explore the passion, the pain, the noise and the power that we hear when we lose that insulation. It is frightening to leave home.

To shore up his strength, Moses said to God, "Look God, you want me to go to the power, and you want me to free the people. Who shall I tell them has sent me?" God said, "Tell them I am who I am." How's that for nourishment? See what that feeds in you. See how that nourishes your sense of power. "I am who I am." What is that?

But when you leave home, and when you begin your spiritual pilgrimage, you are not certain what will feed you. You are not certain there is anything out there that will take your fear and transform it into love. "I am who I am." But friends, the reluctant pilgrims of the Bible have always been people who were willing to go, stripped of their security, trusting to go with a God who is only who God chooses to be.

It is scary, and it leaves you empty. It leaves you so empty that you have to continue exploring the fire. You have to continue exploring where it is leading you.

Have you ever wondered why people go to cemeteries to visit the dead? It is because there is a fire that we do not want to die. There is an emptiness created as our identity is consumed, and that emptiness takes a long time to fill sometimes. That spiritual journey, for most of us, is a lifetime.

It took Moses about forty years to fill the empty space created by taking a people out of their security and wandering around in the wilderness suffering in pain. They did not know where their bread was going to come from. They had to accept the emptiness of uncertainty. It took about forty years. But that is the way it is on a spiritual pilgrimage.

It is the invitation to explore where you meet God, even if there is not a book anywhere that will tell you how to get along with God. It is continuing to explore the passion. It may be a passion created by pain and loss, or it may be a passion to simply live, to dance, to sing, and to develop that gift that is in you, that is burning within you to be lived. Whatever it is, the spiritual pilgrimage is the pursuit of that passion.

Judging from what I see when I stand up here, many of you lived with me in front of television sets having our evening dinner as Walter Cronkite served us up pain and war. As we watched the anguish of the Vietnam War and watched our young come home in body bags, many of you experienced the burning napalm that stripped a countryside, a napalm that stripped us. It cleared our eyes of idealism as we saw the suffering. That searing suffering and burning makes a permanent scar on our souls. It did on mine.

What do you do with the pain? In 1987 I went to Vietnam and Cambodia on a mission. It was called a church mission, but there was something more. It was a mission for my soul. It was a mission to go and be present with those who had suffered there. Fifteen years after the end of the war, we visited that land where terror and holiness merge. We visited those places where we were on the edge of fear and adventure and courage. We keep exploring the burning mystery.

September 11 stripped us of our illusion of privilege and safety. We are wandering in the wilderness, wondering who we are. What does our passport now say about who we are? But we keep going back and visiting the Vietnam War monument. When I go to Washington, D.C., I go to that granite rock wall in the ground, and I take shoes off of the feet of my soul. I walk down into that descending rock, and I look up at the names of 58,000 of my contemporaries who are frozen in adolescence. I go, and I weep, longing to know the sacred in this life. I long for home, where God is.

If you take a spiritual pilgrimage, it takes courage to leave home. But when you leave and explore your passion, trust that the God who is who God is will be with you and help you along the way find a new home.

2

Where Pulpit and Life Meet

This book has been in the works for several years. It has been a slow and sometimes aching process to surface and share my truth. I have struggled to find a voice for my understanding of the preaching life. But my refrigerator door holds a word of grace that helps me understand the laborious process: "Truth, like love and sleep, resists an approach too intense." My truth could not be forced. It had to be nurtured within a context in which it was free to discover and speak itself.

Ideas, like fruit, grow in the soil of experience, fertilized by thoughts and feelings. They are watered by the rain of painful pleasure and passion with people in relationship. To pick the fruit too soon is to contort the mouth in a bitter sour wrinkle. To pick it too late is to lose it to the birds or to taste a sweet sick mush of looming rot. Some who read this book will find the ideas unripe and bitter, while others will say the insights are overripe and should have been left to the birds. Some will taste too much of the earthy soil that feeds the ideas, while others will want the ground to be filtered by more water and light. But this book has come to fruition in its own time, and it is offered for the nourishment it can provide. The ideas in this book have been soaking in soil plowed with the passion of pain and pleasure, and they have been watered by the evaporating rain of time.

The ideas and thoughts shared in this book come from a story of life. This story (like all stories) begins with an ending. I had been preaching weekly for over thirty years when on May 13, 1995, my confidence in the power of the detached word received a fatal wound. At 7:00 p.m., my wife of thirty-one years died. Cancer, which I had only known as infecting people in my congregations, had stolen my wife from me. It had made my children motherless and deeply scarred her parents' hearts.

As I went into the deep spaces of empty agony and mourning, I discovered the power of the body to swallow words. Raging fleshy grief sucked the breath out of words and when I had finished the journey, my words sounded like noisy gongs and clanging symbols. My words were hollow, and I could not find any confidence in them.

The words that haunted me most were words central to the Christian faith that had been my bread and butter. I had spoken with confidence in the love of God in Christ Jesus from whom I could never be separated. But then I sat in the ashes of my life and felt completely deserted by God. I had preached with passion about the ability of humans to make a difference in this world—to be agents for life—but now sat powerless to fend off the relentless pursuit of death. I had preached of the power of prayer to impact the human journey, but now wept powerless with all who suffer as pain eats away at those we love.

The world of understanding that I had constructed and called theology began to fall apart. I had spent my life studying the texts of the faith and reading thousands of books. I thought I had a good understanding of how the human experience and the divine mystery were related. I had enough light on that relationship to find comfort and hope in my life. The dark corners of mystery were stuffed in the closet, and I went on speaking as if darkness did not exist.

But when all the words and understandings I had accumulated over fifty-two years of living were swallowed in one breathless moment of death, disappearing in return of life to dust, doubt in the role of words and concepts multiplied exponentially.

This loss of confidence was devastating for one who had made his living with words. A preacher is one who has skill at stringing words together to move, motivate, or inform the listener. To be an effective preacher, a person spends endless hours reading words of others, commenting on words of others that some have called sacred. Reading and listening to words of the ancients is a central activity of a preacher. It is the pastor/preacher's call to hear people from the congregation scream words of anger and pain and whisper inaudible prayers of longing.

But the loss of my trust in words made preaching even more challenging than it had always been. It was all I could do to stand up and speak about things that mattered. Bookstores and libraries, long my sanctuary of grace and knowledge, became places where my stomach struggled to stay upright in my belly. I spent my days trying to grieve and care for myself. But I could not do the work I needed to do while serving as a pastor.

So I left the parish twelve years ago and joined a seminary faculty. I was granted the privilege of sharing with students what congregations had spent thirty years teaching me. I shared my journey with other clergy who longed for vitality and life and who struggled each week with words.

In this new role, I was forced the rethink what I believed about words and communication. Eventually I was able to explore words again. I was asked to teach an introductory course on preaching, and I needed to discover what I really believed about it. I have worked to figure out how I might preach again with integrity. It was difficult to stand up before people who long to hear words of hope or healing and doubt the capacity of words to do either. It was difficult to convince others of the efficacy of what I believed when I doubted the ability of words to achieve that task. If I was to teach others to develop the capacity to communicate the stories of faith with confidence, I had to come to my own truth about preaching that was reflective of my more recent life journey.

The result of that journey is in this book.

In creating the course on preaching, I had to be honest about my struggle with words. I concluded that words alone do not have power. If preaching has something to do with conversion, transformation, reformation or change, it is not words that make that happen. I have come to believe that it is relationships that change us. As I have lived these past twelve years, shining a flashlight into the dark mystery of life and suffering, I have come to believe that real transformation takes place only in relationships of persons to other persons and persons in relation to the created order. Words that serve these relationships are words that have power. When I think about the things that have had lasting impact on my life, I believe that I have been changed more by relationship to persons than by ideas that I have been given or thought.

I have discovered this by reflecting on the people who helped me reword my life and learn to speak with a new voice. I teach in a seminary and have been blessed with relationships with colleagues who listened patiently as I struggled to make words again. People asked me to preach again, knowing that the words I would speak might be dripping with doubt and confusion. Students graciously struggled to understand and probe the deeper questions of faith and ministry. They helped me speak the truth that was emerging inside of me.

But one of the most powerful relationships that helped change my doubt into confidence was my relationship with the woman who became my wife, Deborah. A woman who loves exploring meaning in life and language, she loved me in my suffering and invited me to play with words with her. One of the ways she did this was to send me an e-mail, which was a verse of a poem she wrote. She then asked me to write a verse of the poem. She wrote:

> She rose early having given in to the gentle nudging of
>   the day's promise.
> Soon.
> Soon, he would be there armed with a slow smile and a
>   quiet voice,
> Adventure suits them. Unknown treasures to be
>   unearthed…

I replied:

> Some are sharp, rusted and hard to touch, others soft and
>   new
> but they sift and sort, feeling and tasting to know what is
>   real.

> Some will be remembered and woven into each soul,
>   others will be
> recovered
> for a day when they can be touched again.

And she wrote:

> Time, the third companion,
> wove electric threads of memories unspoken—
> stitching present to past
> with a watch pointing North.

This relationship with Deborah, filled with words that gently evoked heart and soul, began to open me up to the life that was mine to live. My relationship with Deborah was a way of being changed and, at the same time, a way words were revived in my life.

As this relationship grew, I came to believe that the healing of the human heart is more likely facilitated by relationships rather than simply through thought and ideas. I have come to believe that the ultimate healing of our souls, or salvation as some would call it, is the result of right relationship with God. I believe that our deepest wounds are healed by our relationship with God. We humans have a longing to be connected to the holy. Some would say we long to be reunited with the power of life that creates us. To be reconciled to that life is to be reconciled to the divine life within creation and within the creatures of this planet. When we are one with that life-giving creative power that breathes all into existence, our breath breathed through the words we speak becomes a healing presence.

Now to say this does not mean that I do not value words. But I value them more as vehicles that communicate personhood than things of value themselves. I believe that preaching is more a matter of facilitating healing relationships than communicating information, as information does little to transform us. I think of relationships not only with people who have shared my experiences of change with me, but also people whose stories of self-revelation have revealed new dimensions of me.

Some believe that we are changed by what we believe. They spend a lifetime struggling to define right belief because they are confident that believing correctly will save them, will heal the breach between them and the divine and somehow guarantee an abundant life.

Some therefore think that preaching is to help people come to right belief. They operate on the assumption that salvation, reconciliation, and healing happen by believing right things. I once thought the same. I spent a good deal of my life struggling to speak words that encouraged right belief. It seemed to me that if people could see the truth of what I was saying, they could change their lives to conform to that truth. I passed along all the information I could find to convince them to believe the truth I believed.

But I now wonder how much the information I shared actually changed people's lives. I wonder if the information not only failed to transform them, but may have actually functioned to perpetuate the illusion that we can control our lives and change ourselves at will. Our confidence in information is related to our desire to be in charge of our own lives and to manage the mystery that permeates anything that is alive. We can hide from the mystery with enough information.

Others believe that healing of the breach between the divine and created order is facilitated by right worship. They believe that the practices of the liturgy carry the healing connection with the divine. Liturgy, the work of the people, becomes the means by which we can become one with God.

But I now believe that worship can become a substitute for our encounter with God. By emphasizing the experience of God in worship, we develop some expectation of how God will appear. We go to worship expecting to encounter the holy one and when the encounter does not produce what we had expected in us, we are disappointed. Feeling God in worship does very little to transform our relationship with the God who lives in the created world where decisions about justice and love are made moment-by-moment. The experience of worship becomes a "stand-in" for encountering God, who comes to us in the raw struggle of real life in intimate relationships, politics, and ecology.

Some think right belief heals us, and others believe that right worship heals us. Still others believe that salvation is in the journey of discovery of truth. They open themselves to the diverse belief systems of the world, often finding insight and healing in discovering some truth consistent with life experiences and inherent in all belief systems.

This leads people to desire preaching that is an intellectual cafeteria of diverse insights and ideas. They want preaching to be intellectually interesting and challenging, offering them many flavors to pick from. They want the freedom to hear and select the flavor of the month that satisfies their desire to understand themselves at this point in their journeys. The words they hear from the preacher are gifts of insight.

But knowing more does not necessarily result in living differently. A media-hungry world where people get more and more information does not necessarily result in more just and loving behavior. Sometimes the cafeteria of information becomes a rancorous cacophony of noise and dissonance with people shouting their truth at each other as if that would change peoples' minds and thus change them.

I believe that healing of fractured relationships with the divine occurs not because one believes right, worships right, or finds truth within multiple systems. Salvation comes as a result of being in relationship with God through living flesh—being in relationship to the characters of faith, both those who live among the saints and those who live among us in this world. This assumption is grounded in the understanding of the incarnate divine reality. It is consistent with the understanding that the divine is revealed in human, creaturely nature. God, who creates and recreates reality, abides in particular, unique creatures.

Therefore, the preaching that I recommend works to facilitate healing relationships. It assumes that each relationship is unique and therefore the discovery of the divine reality within those relationships is unique. Preaching does not presume to tell others what the relationships means. My relationship with my wife, Deborah, means one thing to her and another to me. For me to tell her that the meaning of our relationship must be seen the way I see it is to limit my experience of the divine, which is revealed in her particular way of seeing the divine in our relationship. To suggest that either of us has the right way of seeing the relationship is to assume that one of us has an inside understanding of what reality is, and that there is a correct way of knowing the meaning of our relationship.

To preach with the assumption that each relationship is unique changes the spirit of the preaching experience. When we preach with the goal of helping people connect to each other and when we do not assume that we can explain the meaning of that connection, we free ourselves to *enjoy* preaching and *enjoy* the relationships. We free ourselves from the compulsion to come up with something that is right. We express our trust in the work of the spirit to make of the complex and confusing reality of life and relationships that which God might use for the blessing of the world.

Now some people fear this way of working with the stories from scripture. They believe that too much freedom in relationships will open the church to approve of any thing. They believe that the church does not have the luxury of time to nurture saving relationships. They believe that there are too many dangers in the world, and that people must be alerted to those dangers. They believe that their understanding of tradition must be passed on because it holds the secret for right living. They are confident that the church does not have time to facilitate healing relationships.

And their understanding is reasonable. When we look around us and see actions destructive to the spirit of grace revealed in our life with Jesus, we feel compelled to correct them for the sake of those caught up in the destructive behavior. If we see someone caught in an abusive relationship with a child for example, we are compelled to do what we can to stop that relationship. Some actions must be declared wrong, and we must have ways to enforce the boundaries to protect the innocent and the weak.

I would not quarrel with this understanding. But what I would suggest is that preaching from this perspective *alone* puts the preacher and the congregation in the position of law enforcement rather than in developing ways for people to be healed in their relationship with the divine in the other. It makes the pulpit a bully authority designed to extend control over the behavior of the listener, rather than the mediator of a relationship freedom with a divine energy that can transform the heart and soul of the listener.

When one goes to a play by William Shakespeare, one is invited into relationships with the characters and encouraged to discover what the complex emotions and actions of the characters represent. You have the freedom to do this because Shakespeare does not function as a moralist. He gives you enough information about the characters and their situations to help you understand them so that you can identify with them. But you as the listener have the enviable freedom to develop your own feelings about the characters and their decisions.

To assume each relationship is unique is also to conjecture that the relationship is historically conditioned. How we respond to a relationship today may differ from how we will respond tomorrow. Each time you see a play you may arrive at a different understanding of each of the characters. Lady Macbeth is one who is not usually held up as a model of virtue. But sometimes in our lives we are so angry and frustrated with others that we have the emotions she expresses and have at least a better understanding of what might have motivated her actions.

Preaching the Bible is the same. The stories of people in the Bible are not there to be models for how we should live. They are not a paradigm of right and wrong. But they are characters as complex and confusing as any of us, engaged with the holy and aching to know what that engagement means. They become witnesses to the consequences of engaging the terrible holy one in human life. We live with the saints in both their actions that result in serving divine justice and love, as well as the actions that result in violating divine grace and justice. Our role as preachers is to use language that represents these people honestly and thereby allow their unique encounters with the listener to develop into divine activity.

In preaching we must respect not only the differences in the lives of our ancestors, but also in the listeners. They have different contexts in life, and we must allow them to develop their own understanding of the relationship with God and what it means.

Preaching that allows this and also respects the centuries of understanding developed by the church can be done by suggesting to people that there are *diverse* ways of understanding the meaning of some character's relationships to the church and the world. Yet the preacher shares these as helpful hints from relationships that others had with this particular character. For us to preach to facilitate a relationship between the listener and Jesus, it is helpful to get some different pictures from commentators on the meaning of Jesus for them and for others in antiquity. This means that the four gospel portraits of Jesus must be presented in their differences. They must not be blended to get one clear and consistent image. To do that is to discount the different ways unique individuals perceive Jesus.

Preaching that wants to explore the relationship between life and belief has to be grounded in the life out of which belief grew. If a preacher wants to help people engage in forgiving activity, that can best be done by sharing stories of people who struggle to forgive. This will enable people to develop a forgiving attitude more effectively than if we simply exhort them to forgive those who might have hurt them.

The same is true with those who believe that healing comes through relationship to the liturgy. The liturgy is the work of the people. When preaching is couched in the body of the saints in their particularity and in their uniqueness, the listener can relate to real humans who are touched by the grace of divine memory. This is the strength of churches that celebrate different saints each week throughout the year. The worshippers hear their own lives couched in the lives of those faithful to their holy encounter in the past.

I therefore believe that preaching is the sharing of stories of living and sainted persons in such a way that the listener gets to know them. Each listener will get to know the persons shared in sermons differently, for each listener is unique. No one can tell us the personal impact or meaning of any other person to us. So the integrity of the persons introduced is important. This book will explore how to allow individual integrity and diversity to shape these relationships.

I will show how this way of preaching will be effective in the diversity of personalities in a congregation. I will share insights as to how to communicate respect for the mystery of divine reality embodied in persons so that preaching is not an oversimplification of life.

Because of the nature of preaching as facilitating relationships, this book is not a classic "how-to" book. As each relationship is unique, no one can tell us how to be in relationship. I will describe the landscape of relationships and how preaching might be seen as facilitating people to be in relationships, but I will not be able to walk with each preacher and each person they are introducing to people in the congregation. The preacher's own relationship with the biblical characters and persons in the congregation will define the peculiarities of how the sermon will be developed.

I will explore this concept of preaching by first looking at the way relationships function to change, transform, heal and save us (chapter 4). I will then explore the contexts for preaching (chapter 6). Chapters 8, 10, and 12 will develop a strategy for creating sermons that honor the relational dimensions of transformation and healing. Interspersed throughout the book are different sermons that illustrate the material developed in the book. The "Postlude" is an essay first published in *The Living Pulpit* [1] serving as a metaphor for the way preaching as facilitating healing relationships can be imagined visually.

3

The Strangely Familiar

Jn. 20:11–18

To begin any pilgrimage, one must leave home. As with Moses, there is no way to get from where we are to where we want to be without the courage to leave that which is familiar and comfortable. But most of us are reluctant pilgrims because it is hard to leave home. Even if the home is painfully abusive or empty of love, it is not easy to leave.

To begin any spiritual pilgrimage, one must have the courage to leave the safe spaces of the sacred surroundings in which one is sustained. Most of us are reluctant pilgrims when it comes to our spiritual journeys because even empty plates are less frightening than no plates on the table at all. Familiar words have a ring of truth long after they are empty of any truth at all.

But something in each human heart longs for more than empty words.

There is something in each of us that wishes to row out into the mystery and have the courage to lay down the pinochle cards in the bottom of the boat. There is something that seeks more. And even if we do not seek to grow or yearn to move away toward something greater and deeper, sometimes home leaves us and we have no choice. Sometimes we are left alone without the sustaining support of that which is familiar.

Mary Magdalene lost her home. She had known the home only a time. For her, being with Jesus created a sense of home. We do not know a lot about Mary Magdalene, but we do know that she was not well respected within her community. She was one who lived on the edge of home most of her life. No one much embraced her except for the service of their own passions. (Listeners chided me for my depiction of Mary Magdalene; see chapter 4) No one called her by name, but Jesus did. And in the company of those who walked with Jesus, she found herself. She knew her name. She was loved, and that is what it is to be at home. But home left Mary. Jesus died. Jesus died, abused and beaten as a criminal. Her friend and home died and disappeared into cave, a tomb.

When your home dies, you have no choice but relearn your world. You have no choice but to learn how to live again in the absence of that which you have known to be a sustaining presence. You must grieve. Grieving is the process of relearning our world. In the world of rapid change in which we live now, most of us spend our lives trying to catch up and relearn our world.

I cannot tell you how many times I have called my secretary to my office to say, "This computer… This computer, what's wrong with this computer?" And she explains it and goes back to her office, and a week later I call, "What's wrong with this computer?" I cannot keep up. Home keeps disappearing. To live in our world is to learn to grieve and to be in a constant state of relearning how to live. But where do we go to learn how to live?

Mary went to a tomb. Mary went looking for the one who named her and who gave her a home. Mary's first place to go was where she believed there was at least the presence, even if it was dead, that had known her. She went to a sacred site.

That is what sacred sites are. They are places profoundly rich with memory, life, death, power, terror, love, and passion— so rich with memory that we have to keep going back until the memory speaks its sacred word to us, until we learn from that place and its presence the courage to live again.

Last February I went to New York City. I remember walking down Park Avenue. It was a strange sensation to be in the city that I love with the memory of September 11 hanging over me. I walked down the street. I looked in the faces of police officers, sanitation workers, secretaries, and executives. An interesting thing appeared. On the forehead of each of these persons was a black smudge over the eyebrow. It was Ash Wednesday. As I walked back past St. Patrick's Cathedral, I could not help but remember those running, terrorized people bathed in ashes.

And I had to go to Ground Zero. Something seduced me to that site. I had to go.

There is something about it. The terror, the power, the courage, the love, the death—there is something about the power of life and death as they merge in cataclysmic ways that draws us back. We go because we cannot comprehend. That is what a sacred place is. It is a place that is so packed with memory and power that it is incomprehensible. We keep going back.

In my journey I have discovered that some of us who lost our partners have much in common with those who lost their jobs, or their partners in divorce, or their children, or their faith. We keep going back to figure out what it is in that life before that will inform us, shape us, and help us relearn our world. We keep returning to sacred places. That is where Mary went—to a tomb—a sacred place.

Worlds fade and disappear. Home evaporates. A wedding party, family and friends, and all of a sudden a human bomb goes off in the midst of the party, and home is gone. A Palestinian mother sits beside the empty bed where her son who blew himself up used to sleep, and home is gone. We have to relearn our world.

Mary did this by going to a monument. John says when she went to the tomb, it was still dark. When John talks about time and geography, he is not primarily speaking literally. When he says it is dark, he means something more than the time of day. He means it is dark in the heart. It is so dark the heart cannot see. So often, spiritual pilgrimages begin in the dark. They begin when we cannot imagine where we are going, when we are confused. They begin when we are unable to assess our own lives and discover our own strength. They begin in the dark.

Sometimes the darkness becomes a friend. My pilgrimage began in the dark. When my world came unglued I did not understand. I sought the dark. I sought the night. I was awake in the night and wanted to sleep in the day, as the day was too bright. It was the night, the music of the night that seduced me. There is something about the night. There is something about the dark even when you are scared.

In the midst of leaving home, the darkness can be intensely black and frightening, but sometimes it is friendly. Sometimes you simply want to let the darkness embrace you and hold you, because you do not want to see or decide. When it is dark, nobody expects you to do anything.

Mary went to the tomb in the dark, and she wept as she stood at the tomb. She wept. And there was a friendly stranger nearby who said, "Whom are you looking for?" (Jn. 20:15) *The* question when you leave home, "What are you looking for?"

Some months after my first wife died, I was on the road all the time. I was leaving town and disappearing. My adult children did not know how to get in touch with me. Finally, a friend who has the courage to speak honestly with me said, "Moseley, what the hell are you looking for?" I said, "I don't know. I don't know what I'm looking for."

When most of us begin our spiritual journey, it is dark, and we are not certain what we are looking for. But we have a hunch. And my hunch bore itself out as time went along. I have finally decided that Mary and I were looking for the same thing. Mary said, "I'm looking for Jesus. I want to know where they put him." That is, she was looking for home. But when you are looking for home, what you are really looking for is yourself. You are really looking for what disappeared, for that which helped you know who you were. You are looking for yourself. Every spiritual journey is a journey inward to discover who we are.

But Mary could not see who was asking her the question. She could not see the familiar stranger because of her tears, her pain, and her fear. She could not see the one who had created home for her, who was there in another way. She could not see. Why is it that we cannot see those who are familiar when we have left home? It is because when we leave home, the first stranger we meet is ourselves. We really do not know who we are, and, therefore it is extremely difficult to see the other as before.

When I was seeking home, I traveled to Alabama to see my daughter, Kimberly, and her son, John. I got anxious when I went to see them. There was an anxiety in me that was not there before. There was a fear, a frustration, and I did not know what it was. I thought it might have been the fact that while my wife and I were visiting in Alabama, she had gotten very sick toward the end of her life. I thought, well maybe, when I go to Alabama, I will remember *that* experience and *that* pain.

But a therapist helped me see that that was not the only thing it could be. He said, "Your problem may be that you have never been a parent to your daughter without your wife." All of a sudden it became clear. I was the stranger, and through these strange eyes, I was looking at my familiar daughter and seeing a stranger. As I thought about it, I realized that she, too, was looking through strange eyes for she had never been a motherless child.

When we leave home, it is hard to see even the familiar, and thus, it is very frightening. But Mary stayed at the tomb. The disciples had come, and they had looked. And what did it say about these male disciples? They went home. Some of us men are so anxious to get home that we do not stand around sacred centers very long and weep. But Mary stayed. Mary stayed in that strange place where she felt herself to be a stranger. She stayed long enough to hear a strange gardener say, "Mary." (Jn. 20:16) She stayed long enough to hear the voice of her home call her name.

Sacred pilgrimages take time—a lot of tears, a lot of loneliness, and a lot of fear that comes from that which feels so strange and unusual. But when we stay long enough, we may just hear our name.

If you are a parent, you spend much of your life protecting your children. You do not want them to hurt. You try to protect them from some of the severe and painful issues around you. You turn off the television when you see awful things happening to people. You want to protect your children from pain.

I was that kind of parent. I did not like to share some of the painful truth about my life with my children. But I have discovered that my children have always known me better than I thought they did. On my journey through loss, I got to the point where I had no energy left to protect my children from my pain.

I finally made a telephone call to each of my children and I said, "Look, I'm exhausted. I'm lost. And I don't know if I can be of help to you right now. I need you to help me. Can *you* hold *me* for a little while?"

And they did. Each of them drew upon the resources that were in them, looked through their tear-stained eyes and studied this strange man who was their father. They each looked at me again, and I heard each of them speak my name. I was still "Daddy," but now, I am also "Dan."

4

How Relationships Heal and Transform

Transformative Theology

Preaching is an art form practiced primarily within the context of congregational worship. Therefore, if preaching is to have integrity, it must serve the larger purpose of congregational life, which is to facilitate reconciliation between God and creation and between creatures. This purpose of the Christian community is affirmed by the writer of Ephesians, who describes the work of God as bringing divided people together with each other and with the divine self (Eph. 2:11–22). Our role is to facilitate relationships that witness to the divine power of reconciliation. When we do this, we not only proclaim divine power but become that power at work in all creation to contribute to God's healing work. We contribute to a fuller, more abundant life.

What does healing mean? To be healed is to be connected with that which enhances wholeness. It is to be in relationship with that dimension of spirit that integrates the diverse dimensions of self and world into a pattern of relating that brings justice and peace to those who cohabit this planet. We call it *peace* or *shalom.* But it is a reconciling relationship with creation, creator, and creatures that enhances the possibility of wholeness.

Healing occurs when we are changed, and change occurs when we are healed. It is relationships that change us. This is consistent with the theology the church proclaims. We believe that God relates to humans in flesh. That is the meaning of the Incarnation. God's way of connecting with and working to heal creation is through humans. In Jesus, God reveals the divine character and how that character challenges limited understandings of creation and expands them to be more whole and loving.

The church has known that we are made whole through relationships. Pentecost was the experience of diverse people becoming church through relationships. It was people being changed by the presence of diverse people from around the world. It was the experience of being changed from people who could not understand each other to people who could hear and understand in their own tongues.

People who work with children know that relationships make them who they are. Relationships with loving and trusting parents contribute to children becoming loving and trusting. But if a parent violates the child's trust, the child may become fearful and less capable of bonding.

People addicted to certain behavior know that the relationships they have either contribute to their addictions or help them overcome them. When people try to change addictive behavior, they have to change the community of people they hang with. It is not enough that they want to change themselves. Being with people who encourage healthy behavior is critical to becoming transformed.

People who have ever made New Year's resolutions know this. Most of my life I have noble beginnings to the new year. I consider the things that I want to do better, and I make a list. The first week I am good at functioning differently. The second week I slack off. By the third week, my old patterns take over, and I am left with little change and a lot of guilt. Why is it so hard to change?

Barriers to Transformation

Change includes loss. Our memory system struggles with giving up that which has helped define who we are. We can intellectually affirm that the action of God is to make all things new. We can cognitively believe that God's will is emerging with a future that looks like the great banquet where all are welcomed and none are turned away. We can say, as my mother taught me to do, "This is the day that the Lord has made. Let us rejoice and be glad in it." (Ps. 118:24) We can believe what quantum physic teaches, that all is simply in process and that each moment is completely new–it has never been before. We can assent to statements that this moment is new and that this matrix of people, places, emotions, and futures has never been aligned this way before.

We can intellectually embrace these ideas and still be unable to live differently. I was hiking in the woods and met a man and woman who were strolling and visiting. As with most conversations that I hear on the trail, I heard only a snippet of it. The woman said to the man, "I know in my logical mind that it doesn't help to worry, but…" I do not know what she was talking about, but because I know how hard it is to give up worry, I suspect she was talking about concern for her children, or for the upcoming visit to the doctor, or for the threat of a layoff, or any number of other circumstances. This woman understands intellectually the man's suggestion, "It doesn't do any good to worry," but she worries nonetheless.

What is it about the self that builds a barrier between what we know in our heads and what we are inclined to do? Where is the great divide?

I believe that our past relationships have a profound impact on our ability to become new creatures. We have cognitive memories and experiences that our subconscious remembers. We also have precognitive memories that live deep within the soul that influence our response to a given situation. The soul makes up the spiritual DNA of the body, and there is memory in the body that does not forget just because the mind does not retain information. Some physical therapists say that the body remembers every pain that it has had. I would suggest that the mind, body, heart, and soul all remember the pain and anxiety of loss and that those memories are frequently engaged when we are challenged to make changes.

So to simply give people the idea that God desires that they become different creatures does not create in them the energy to change. The past is not past—it lives on inside the body and soul of the believer.

So to help overcome the barrier to transformative behavior, we need to evoke from the memory of the listener the presence of people who live in that past and who might empower them to risk new behavior. We must evoke in them the fearful voices, the people within the internal memory who whisper danger and fear. Those voices must be spoken. Maybe by hearing these voices we can disempower them, allowing us to hear other voices from within that might speak courage.

I have discovered this in my struggle to write something longer than a sermon. When I take time to explore my difficulty in writing, it comes down to a fundamental fear of saying the "wrong" thing. Early childhood experiences contribute to that. The people in the constellation of my soul worry about saying the wrong thing. They caution me to speak carefully.

For me to be free from their control, I must hear them. I must be around people who can help me hear them for what they are. It helps to have people around me who can mimic those voices so I can recognize them. When I hear them now, I can hear them not as the child I was when I first heard them, but as the sixty-five-year-old adult that I am now.

And when I let those fearful voices speak from my soul, I can face that fear as a grown man. I open myself to the point of fear of abandonment and rejection that once accompanied the use of "wrong" words. I can remember other voices and listen to other people within my soulful constellation who did not reject me for "being wrong." I can then begin to listen to artists and writers who live in my memory and who say those same words and are not rejected. I can open to the memory of being taught that the creator loves me and calls my creation good. I can imagine that that creator can use even my "wrong" words to bless because I have in my memory a relationship with Jeremiah who, when he was told by God that he was to be a prophet to the nations, replied, "Ah, Lord God! Behold,

I do not know how to speak, for I am only a youth." (Jer. 1:6, RSV).

For me to be healed and freed and to become a person who lets words out for others to read, I need to be in relationship with people in my contemporary world. For my voice to be expressed, I need to be in relationship with people in my cognitive *and* precognitive memories whose presence is steadfast and loving regardless of what I think or what I say. For me to be healed, I must hear both the words within me that trigger my fears as well as those that empower me to write and speak myself into the world.

When this is done, I open up to a larger realm of understanding from which I can draw as I seek to respond to the current situation. Having more options gives us a chance to make a more appropriate response.

Another barrier to our changing and being open to transformation is the way we respond to the parental preaching patterns that seem to dominate many of our churches. As a former pastor of congregations and now a faculty member at a seminary, I have many opportunities to visit churches and listen to people preach. I also teach preaching, and I am blessed with multiple occasions to hear students preach. Most preaching that I hear seems to believe in the gospel of "working harder." Almost every sermon I hear implies that I must change the way I am living and that if I only work harder, I can change into that which God expects me to be. It even seems that divine grace requires that I work harder to get it.

One of the problems with preaching is that preachers assume that information and hard work will change people. If people know that Jesus is a good man and understand how his life can enhance contemporary life, they may very well be persuaded to change the way they live. And we often live our way into a new way of being. Sometimes practice can change perspectives and changed perspectives can change the way we live our lives.

However, most of us find it very difficult to live in a new way if we are not supported and reinforced by people around us. The systems in which we live have a stake in our remaining the same. So for us to decide that we are going to change without regard to the power of the relationships around us sets us up for failure. The internal systems that form us as we are create strong resistance to our changing and becoming a different person.

Transformative Preaching

Transforming experiences in life are not so much ones where we know information about something, but are the ones where we are known by someone. To be known and to know is to be on the inside. And being inside of something impacts us and changes us, rather than our being in control of the change.

It is those experiences that are bigger than our mind can comprehend or our lives can control that change and transform us at some deep and abiding level. I made this discovery when I became a father. I lived most of my early years as a father with the illusion that I could understand my children and therefore make decisions in their best interest. But the dynamics between parent and child are much greater than the mind can understand. Even when I read dozens of books on raising children, I discovered that there was something unique about my relationship with each of my children that made our lives together a mystery. And even when I could understand something, the dynamics of our love and our interconnection kept me from being able to control everything.

I was changed by my relationships to persons who were unique and mysterious. I was changed by dynamics formed and shaped by the unique mystery of each of us and of us together. I was not transformed into a father by reading about how to do it and by working hard at it; but rather by being attentive to the people around me and by allowing myself to be inside the relationships and be affected by them.

Since it is relationship to God through our relationship to others that is the transforming power in life, preaching should be about facilitating relationships. It should help people discover the divine presence in both friend and stranger. The biblical stories are about how God's presence is embodied within the character and memory of the tribe or the congregation. People were created as the people of Israel by living in relationship to the family history and memory. People became church by singing, praying, and eating together.

Yet the biblical stories are not simply about being formed by our relationship with friends and family. They are also about being touched by the divine in the stranger and the enemy. God called the ancient Hebrew people to live with kindness to the stranger because they had once been aliens who were welcomed by strangers. God encouraged them to welcome strangers for in so doing, they would entertain angels unawares. Their enemies were agents of the divine will, creating a context in which God would guide and challenge their future. The early Christian people also were encouraged to welcome strangers for their Lord was revealed to them in people and places that they did not expect.

The preacher's community of friends and strangers is not simply those people who live around us here and now. They are people who surround us in the company of the saints. The people who can offer us healing are people who live and breathe in the world around us, as well as those whose spirits surround us in memory.

If we were to preach as if we trusted these relationships to change and heal us, the spirit with which we come to the pulpit and speak would change. If we were to preach in a way that invited people into relationship with strangers and friends in the community of faith and the community of saints, the listener would not feel burdened with expectations. The listener would be open to getting acquainted with persons who have been significant to the preacher and to the community of which the listener is a part. Prophetic and pastoral preaching are cut from the same fabric. Prophetic preaching is the result of facilitating relationships with people outside ourselves; pastoral preaching occurs when healing relationships are facilitated with those who reside inside us. When we preach to challenge people to do better and to work harder, we push—and some people are not pushed in the direction we want them to go. But if we invite them to gently explore relationships with friends and strangers in their communities of faith, they may be guided into healing relationships.

The Individual Communal

One way I have discovered to gently guide people to explore the way relationships can heal is to look at an individual as a matrix of relationships. We often see individuals as singular. But when I see individuals as communities I understand better the people I work with and myself. Each individual is made up of multiple individuals who have shaped and shape who he or she is. When we are preaching to individuals, there are multiple perspectives within each individual hearing the words of the sermon simultaneously.

In the graphic below, we imagine a person in the pew is the dark X in the middle of the graphic. When a person is listening to a preacher, she is sitting there with multiple companions inside her. She has come to church with a rich, complex historical community that has shaped how she hears the words you speak. For example, if you use the word "God," the listener has many overt and covert memories of what that word means. Many people will have an image of an old man with a white

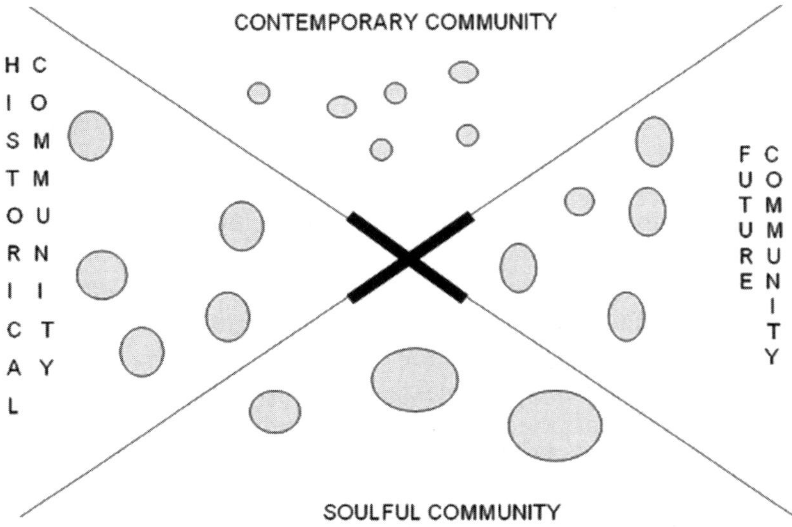

This and subsequent diagrams of the X-Factor first appeared in my book *Living with Loss* (Nashville: Xyzzy Press, 2007).

beard. The word "God" evokes memories of people in church or in the culture using metaphorical language of "father" or "lord" or "creator" or "lover." The listener also may hear voices from his past, reminding him of the character of God as "judging" or "merciful" or "forgiving," or "all-powerful." You place people in touch with their memories of ideas about God and all the people who gave them these symbols and metaphors whenever you use a word from the pulpit. Those relationships shape what and how the listener hears.

Your capacity to help them experience your understanding of God will be directly related to which of the people from their history you help them relate to. For example, if you use the word "father" to refer to God and the person in the pew was abused by his or her father, you will evoke a memory that will not be warm and healing. The voices and memories of those who accompany the person into the sanctuary will shape what they will discover from the sermon that you preach.

Many companions from the contemporary community also accompany a worshiper. The man who sits there is hearing voices from his children who need new shoes. He hears the voice of his boss pressuring him to produce more. He is accompanied by the voices of the political pundits he listened to before he came to church. He hears the voice of the pop singer his children are listening to who admits to multiple sexual encounters before turning sixteen. He hears the voices of the politicians who seek to convince the public that the war is good.

He not only hears the disturbing voices that cry out to him from the culture, but also his wife's whispering love last night when they finally had time for each other. He hears the voice of his dad who called at breakfast today to tell him of the birth of a calf. He hears the laughter of his daughter as she plays with her kitten Muffy. He hears the music of the organ that eases his heart. Those sitting before the preacher are listening not only to the words of the preacher, but to the voices of multiple companions who are ensconced in their hearts.

And the words that are heard take on energy and emotion as they relate to the people who inhabit the listener's life. When the country is engaged in war, the preacher cannot talk about war without evoking the presence of all those people who shape the listener's life. For the preacher to help a person deal with an issue such as war, she must evoke the voices within the listeners that shape their responses to life. She must call forth the voice of the politician who is defending the war. She must bring out the voice of the young soldier who is a paraplegic because a roadside bomb blew up a military jeep. She must evoke the presence of the voices that cry out in songs of protest and those that solicit the presence of mothers who grieve the loss of their children in war. In my sermon "The Strangely Familiar," I reminisce about a journey to New York City in an attempt to evoke the voices of a post-September 11 United States that is at war.

If the congregation is to build healing relationships in our world, the presence of the people who live in the midst of contemporary struggles and chaos must be invoked in the words of the preacher. It is not enough to simply tell people that war is bad and that Jesus is against war. Evoking the presence of people who live among the saints in the past is important. But equally important is calling forth the presence of the real human experiences that people are sharing in this real world of here and now.

The listener sitting in the pew has voices from the saints accompany her to worship. She also has all the voices of the culture and social context crying out to her. But, what she hears the preacher say is also shaped by the companions she brings with her who inhabit her soul (see graphic). When I use this word "soul," it invites many different interpretations. I use this word to refer to the deep spirit and emotions that live below the cognitive memory of the past. When we see an event or hear a word, a deep visceral response often occurs. It is either the consequence of precognitive or physical experiences beyond our mind's capacity to identify the source.

Driving to work recently, I saw an old pick-up truck stopped at a green light. Its hood was protruding into my lane. A disheveled man stood beside the door looking back at an equally-battered pick-up stopped about three feet behind it. A man was leaning out the window of that pick-up. My first response was that of compassion. I sensed that the first truck was stalled and the second truck was being positioned to give it a push. My instinctive, soulful response was one of ease. But then I saw the man in the second truck step out of the truck, stumble, and fall. My soulful response then was alarm—something was wrong with him. But he then got up and started yelling at the man beside the first truck. He was pointing and screaming. The man in the first truck screamed back and made threatening gestures. The subtle voices deep within my soul began to cause a churning in my stomach. My anxiety went up as I realized that they were in a heated argument.

Now I do not know why the people who inhabit my soul responded so differently to each of my perceptions of the situation. But the compassion that turned to alarm and then to anxiety was precognitive. Certain words and events that I experience cause responses that are deep and emotional. In this incident, my soul was listening and responding.

When a preacher is speaking words that evoke memory and feeling, he is inviting into the heart of the listener the people and experiences that are too deep to identify. The soul is filled with experiences that are deep in the bone marrow. They live in the physical memory of the body. When the preacher uses words to help a person discover healing, he needs to be aware of the members of the soul community that live in the persons. I had in mind these memories when my sermon "The Strangely Familiar" described Mary Magdalene's nighttime setting, inviting listeners' own nighttime memories to consciousness.

Sometimes the soul's voices prevent the listener from listening to the preacher. I remember the surprise I had when one of the older members of my congregation came to me to discuss my preaching. He said, "Dan, your preaching doesn't do anything for me." I asked, "What would make it have an impact on you?" He said, "Well, you need to beat me up more!" Somewhere within Frank's soul he had voices that told him that a good sermon must make him feel guilty. Those soulful voices are so deep within us that we cannot know them until they are evoked by experience. They have a profound impact on how people listen to sermons. The listener and the preacher need to develop patience with each other if they are to discover the healing relationships that each desire. The relationship between

Frank and me had to be nurtured before he was able to hear what I had to say in a sermon.

A sermon designed to contribute to transforming a person evokes those voices, not only listening to them but also addressing them. If a preacher is speaking about the joy of giving money to the church, the preacher will be wise to evoke voices from the soul that have nurtured persons as givers. Plenty of voices within the soul speak of fear and scarcity. But there may be voices of tenderness and compassion that come from their early years of receiving undeserved gifts from a grandmother or a friend. In "Strangely Familiar" Mary Magdalene encountered Jesus as one who valued and loved her. Later, after much darkness and waiting, she heard his voice as the one that *did* call her by name. Listeners hearing of Mary's experience with such a loving, naming relationship have the chance to resonate with their own memories, experiences, hopes, and dreams for such loving, naming relationships. Hearing the sound of these loving, naming voices—whether from the experienced past or the imagined future—can contribute to healing of the heart and the community or culture.

As a person listens to sermons at a particular time and place, voices from the past, the present and the soul are shaded and flavored by voices whispered from the future (see graphic). The listener always experiences the voices of "what will be" in the voice of the preacher. These are the unseen and unspoken longings and fears that speak to us about what is not yet.

Voices that are very immediate color the way the words are heard from the pulpit. The voice from the pot roast that is cooking in the oven at home whispers in the ear of the man who is preparing dinner for his family. When the preacher begins her fifth point and the listener sees no end in sight, the pot roast cries out that it is being burned. The voices of the community that gathers for lunch at the local cafeteria after church whisper their concern that there might be a wait if this sermon does not get over soon. These are immediate and powerful voices.

But other voices from the future also color the pictures created by the preacher. If the preacher challenges the listener to give some time to the local food bank in providing food for the homeless, the voices that debate over the use of the listener's valuable time begin arguing. They discuss among themselves whether the listener should spend more time with his son's soccer team or the food bank. Every challenge to the listener to consider a decision to do something with resources for the future evoke the presence of that unnamed, unknown mystery of the not yet.

If the preacher is to be effective in contributing to the changing of the lives of the listeners, he must attend to those multiple whisperings that make claims on that unshaped, undefined space not yet in existence. The preacher must evoke voices of people with whom the listener longs to be connected. He must help the listener hear those voices that affirm her sense of herself.

This is not easy, and it takes time. In the sermon "The Strangely Familiar," I reflect on Mary Magdalene's ability to stand by the tomb, weeping and waiting. It is not easy to stay with our feelings long enough to see what might emerge from the pain of loss. But, when Mary waited in the quiet dark she heard her name called. Deep within her she became aware of a presence that knew her by name—one that knew her in a deep and spiritual way. When the soulful presence has been touched, we are transformed. We are able to leave the place of sadness and make public witness to the power of love that is raised up beyond death.

The community of the individual houses thousands of relationships that shape the way the person listens to the sermon. In each of us, the voices from each of the four quadrants have been organized to create a semblance of equilibrium (see graphic below).

The circle around the center of the quadrant symbolizes the voices that have a dominant place in the construction of a person's sense of self. Most of us listen to the voices from our past, present, soul, and future. These help us negotiate the most immediate concerns of our lives. For example, if I am a parent of small children, the voices I listen to from my past are the ones that help me do parenting the best way I can. The voices that seem to attract the attention of parents from the contemporary community are the ones that address problems with raising young children. The voices I listen to in my soul

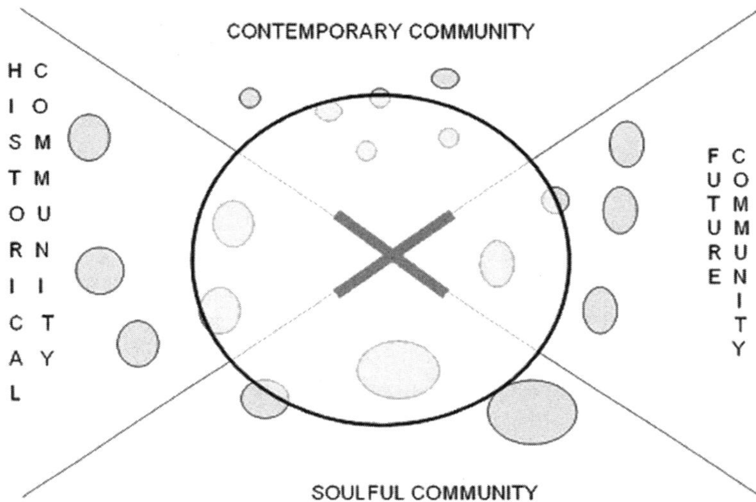

are the ones that help sustain me as I struggle with the deep passions of affection and anger, tenderness and rage. The voices I listen to from the unknown future invite me to improve my ability to be a good parent.

The voices that I will be inclined to ignore are the voices that are outside that circle. I will not be in relationship with voices that raise too many questions about my own desires to fulfill other dreams in my heart. My soul may ache because I am so tired from taking care of children that I do not have energy to deal with my desire to write music. That desire must be quieted if I am going to keep my sanity and maintain a sense of equilibrium.

As a preacher I must be aware that multiple dimensions of a person show up in the sanctuary. If I am going to help a person grow or be more in touch with the divine desire for their lives, I must evoke those voices from within them. I must do it in a way that does not create so much disequilibrium that the listener quits listening. When a person is overcome by too much demand, she will turn away from the one articulating the claim.

After leaving the parish ministry, I had opportunity to visit many congregations and listen to sermons. I was exhausted from grieving multiple losses. Every sermon challenged me to do more than I was currently doing for the sake of the cause the preacher believed was most important. I left each service angry and overwhelmed. It was all I could do at that point to get up and get to church. To be told that I was not doing enough when I thought I was doing all I could manage at that time turned me away from sermons. I was doing the best I could to create some equilibrium within myself and the preacher was trying to open me up to meet other expectations that he thought were important. There was seldom concern for the effort it took for me to listen to the voices outside the circle that defined me.

Preachers need to be aware that there are times in the lives of the listeners when they are listening to more of the voices in the four quadrants than normal. That often happens when the circle of equilibrium is punctured and begins to fly around like a busted balloon. In a time of crisis people are often open to listening to more of their own history than they might have done before (see graphic below).

When I experienced the significant losses in my life and was uncertain about whom I was or who I was becoming, I was more open to strangers around me. I was driven out of the circle of equilibrium and into parts of my past, my present, my soul, and my future to which I had not paid attention. I heard

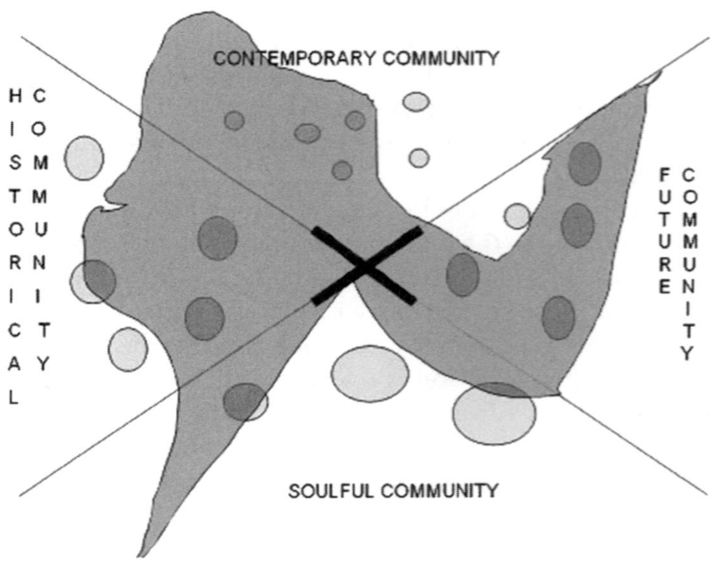

things that I had not heard for a long time. I began listening to the wisdom of the desert mothers and fathers to whom I had been introduced in seminary. I listened to their experiences of a holy absence and found a new way of experiencing holy presence. I had been raised as one who believed in words, and I was drawn to their experience of divine joy in silence. Healing of my spirit began when I opened myself to these strangers from my past and allowed the truth of their presence to minister to me.

I also discovered that attending worship where reason dominated the liturgy and the sermon was not helpful at all. I found myself drawn to those places of worship where confidence in the practice and poetry of liturgy was exhibited by the priest and the people. I listened to contemporary interpreters of the divine reflect the deep influence of eastern philosophy and theology. Because of my fear and my anxiety, being embraced by the tradition reflected in the liturgy comforted me.

I also was driven to listen more deeply to the voices of my soul. These voices, many of which had been silenced by strong influences from parents and the projected expectations of what a minister must be and do, rose up and demanded attention. Anger was one of those voices that resided within my body and soul and that demanded to be heard. The angry music from our pop culture did wonders to draw out the deep anger from within me. I discovered that deep anger and painful passion were the doorway to deep joy and ecstatic pleasure (see chapter 9, "Sacred Memory"). My relationship to the community of the future also changed. I was opened to new voices that I had failed to acknowledge when there was a circle of equilibrium that limited my encounters. I had always assumed that I was be a pastor my whole career. I had been successful and found fulfillment. But when I was living alone for the first time since college and no one depended on my remaining in the same role in the same place, I found that voices from other careers spoke louder to me. I discovered that I listened to people from farther away than the small circle of relationships that had defined my life at that point. I listened to the voices of the unknown future that invited me to consider giving my time and energy to training new leadership for the church.

It was my opening to the people outside the circle in the four quadrants that finally led me to a new sense of self and a new identity. That new sense of self then motivated me to make changes and live in new ways and build relationships with those other parts of myself that could sustain a new way of being. I nurtured those relationships and over years of nurture and practice have become a person who teaches in a seminary.

As I came to believe that relationships are more transforming than ideas, I decided that effective preaching must look at what facilitates relationships. Since I am interested in facilitating relationships that help heal and build up rather than break down, I needed to look at some of the characteristics of healing relationships. When we look at what helps people relate in healthy and healing ways, we can discern some dynamics in sermon preparation that can use the preaching event to contribute to that goal.

In my sermon "Leaving Home," (chapter 1) Moses is cast as someone burning. Moses as a "model leader" could have seemed threatening to people who knew themselves *not* to be model leaders; people who did not have enough time or conviction to become the leaders their congregational culture might have held up as ideal. Moses as an "object lesson doubter" could have seemed a threatening character depiction–giving people the sense that their own faith and doubt levels were being weighed and judged. However, Moses as a wrestling, burning, struggling and limping human offers listeners a space for letting their own confusions and struggles and burnings resonate or burn, not as shameful things but as heroic or valid parts of a faith story. The sermon then functions not so much as a demand for this or that answer. It is then a sacred, cathedral-like space for the questions themselves to burn, possibly unanswered or with no easy answer, for a while (see the "Postlude").

Characteristics of Healing Relationships

We have many kinds of relationships. Some of them heal and some destroy. If we are preaching for healing relationships, we need to consider what a healing relationship is and some of the characteristics of those relationships.

When I talk of healing relationships, I am referring to ways of relating that connect people to the divine sense of wholeness and salvation. Christians believe that creation was intended to be mutually supportive and sustaining. The creation stories in the Bible suggest that God creates all that is and that is all good. The stories also suggest that creation has somehow been alienated from its ultimate intention. It suggests that the work of God has been to bring about shalom: to create a realm of reality in which all creation comes together in peace. God called the prophets to remind people that justice for those who had been shunted to the margins was the primary work of people seeking to serve God's intention for wholeness. Jesus' life opened to all creation and invited his followers to expand their sensitivity and compassion to strangers and enemies, not just to friends. The church was founded as a space where aliens gathered and understood each other. Healing relationships break down barriers of hostility, opening us to more loving and just ways of being companions on the journey of life.

What are some of the characteristics of these relationships?

They Are Loving

Love is the nature of the creator. The biblical stories describe the loving creator as one who gives the divine self to the creatures of the divine hand. They reveal a God who is a companion with the creatures of the earth. The divine presence attends to the creatures with faithful encouragement. Relationships that heal the alienation between God and creation are ones that steadfastly pay attention to the heart of the other.

This loving presence works to facilitate healing of the heart because it assures the creature that she is not alone. The fundamental human fear is that we are alone—that we matter to no one or nothing. The steadfast attention by the Other assures us that we are not alone. We are able to attend to the creation within us and around us because of this faithfulness. We are able to love because we have first been loved. It is this love that helps us not live in fear. Therefore, it is the divine love for creation that frees us to be open to all of the relationships around us.

One of the fundamental barriers to healthy and loving relationships is fear of losing what matters to us. We are afraid of meeting the stranger because if we know and attend to the stranger, that relationship might require that we change the way we do things. If we love a child born into our family, the barrier to attending to his needs is our fear of losing the life we have come to enjoy or appreciate. But if we know the steadfast love of the creator through creatures around us, we can let our fear fade so we can be open to the new life that is available to us because we love the new person in our lives.

They Are Living

In a living relationship each party is alive and changing. Living relationships take courage and sensitivity because someone who is alive is constantly changing and becoming new. They are messy because where life exists, there is change and unpredictability. When my children were young, keeping up with the changes in their lives was all I could do. This was true not only in the constant trips to Sears to buy new shoes and shirts, but also in the struggle to attend to their changing attitudes and capacities. I remember my tension when my daughters went on their first date. I had to continue to adapt and change as they became more experienced in relationships. I had to come to terms with what I could influence and what was out of my control. I had to open myself to their right to be free and struggle with my desire to protect them from pain.

And in those times with my children, we all changed. We all were opened up to more of life than we might have known had we not been relating to each other. They opened me up to a world of young people emerging around me. They opened me to the courage they had to face the unknown, to try new things and discover what worked and what did not. I opened them to some wisdom that had been handed to me by my parents. I opened them to consider responsibility along with impulse, and history along with innovation. By being in a living relationship, we continually changed and discovered a larger and more abundant life than we might have known.

What makes sense in relationships between living humans might not seem to make sense in relationships with those who are in our memory. Many times when we preach, we create fixed images of people. Peter is often presented as a "rock." This sense of fixedness makes it difficult to have a living relationship with Peter. Most of us experience a rock as the same each time we encounter it. It is always there, waiting for us exactly where we left it before. We can use it when we want, and we can ignore it when we want. If we relate to people as fixed and never changing, the relationship we have with them is not alive. It does not have the potential of changing those in the relationship.

The art of preaching that facilitates healing relationships requires that we find ways to present those who live in memory as living realities. It requires that we continually reopen our memories and imagine what the deceased saint might have thought in this new and changing world. It requires that we imagine Jesus in this world, discuss with him what he had to say in the past, and wonder with him if he would say something similar in the situation as we find it today.

They Have Memory

Healing relationships with those who have peopled our world and who live in memory can also contribute to our healing. We can discover the spirit of those memories still breathing in our hearts. Attending to the spirit of their memory can revive those people.

This can often be done in community in ways that help us overcome our fixed caricature of the person in memory. When my mother died, I gathered with my siblings, my children, my nieces and nephews, friends of the family, and we sat around and told stories about our lives with mother. Whereas I remembered some of the incidents we discussed from my perspective, they remembered them from their perspectives. As each reminisced, my sense of my mother's presence expanded. I not only had my own memories to relate to, but the different memories of my family caused me to open myself to a fuller sense of my mother. And my memories, distorted by my own needs and desires, had companions for knowing mother anew. Even as mother had just been buried, her life animated the life of each one of us in ways that we had not known before.

Community memory is a powerful way of helping relationships become living and vital. The church gathering to discuss the saints of antiquity can bring fresh and living awareness to the preacher and to the listeners of sermons. When the community gathers to chew over times of trauma such as the forty years of wandering in the wilderness, the saints of the past come alive. When American citizens gather over coffee to commiserate over our nation's history between the Vietnam War and the most recent war in Iraq, the people who died come alive and speak to us. My sermon "Leaving Home" (chapter 1) seeks to evoke those voices as we explore the longings that set us on reluctant pilgrimages of faith.

Living relationships are ones whose memory still infuses the present. I remember struggling with anger over a conflict in the seminary. My heart was intense, and my focus was narrow. My gut felt like dirty socks roiling in a clothes dryer. As I struggled with my colleagues, I remembered a time when I was sixteen. I was walking with two friends down Broadway in my hometown. A car drove by and Bill, an older student at our school, yelled an obscenity. One of my friends returned the insult and then became fearful that they would come back and confront us. I, feeling foolishly courageous, said, "No, they won't do that," and replaced my friend, walking closer to the street. Then, before I knew what hit me, Bill grabbed me from behind and threw me to the ground, bruising my tailbone. He then ran off. I have remembered that incident from time to time through the years; but within the context of conflict with my colleague in the seminary, I felt a raging anger toward that boy in ways that I had not felt for forty-five years. The different context for that memory created different feelings in me and changed its impact on me. Memories can be living and continue to impact who we are becoming.

They Are Physical

For a relationship with a person to be healing, it must reflect more than a cognitive connection. It must be physical. It must have smell, sound, taste, touch, and sensation. If we are to be impacted by the relationships of our lives, our bodies must be involved. Transformation is a full body experience—not just the transforming of the mind and heart. When what we are related to has a physical presence, it cannot only change the way we think and feel, but must also change what we do.

The physical nature of the relationship gives it power. Preaching that puts me in relationship to my senses enables me to feel a physical presence. I still remember one of the most powerful sermons I have ever heard. I heard it decades ago. Dr. Fred Craddock taught at the university I attended. He preached a sermon, "Doxology," that is still a classic. In it, he gave an idea flesh and blood, made it breathe and walk around. Dr. Craddock led us on a journey in which he takes Doxology to supper, downtown, to visit a sick person with him, and on a vacation. He wondered throughout the sermon whether Doxology should be present in all those places.[1] As one listens to the sermon, one not only thinks about doxology but lives it with joy as one lives sensually the delight of a small playful creature.

Through the use of language that communicates very personal and vivid physical images, Dr. Craddock facilitated my relationship with memories deep in my soul. By his spare but particular use of words, he places me on my patio and makes me feel the night seeping into my heart as the cool of fall tickles my goose bumps. He sends me back to my memories of our dog Honey and her playful presence wherever we were. The spirit of the idea and the spirit of the language both take on physical characteristics and facilitate my relationships with my own experience and my own memories. Because the sermon is so physical, it has a profound impact on my whole sense of self and places me in touch with the spirit of joy and celebration that reflects a presence of divine grace.

They Have Boundaries

Physical relationships are also bound by limits. When we facilitate loving, living, and healing relationships for people, we also help them explore the limits of their humanity. Healthy relationships recognize the boundaries that make us who we are. We do not merge. We are separate and distinct; because of our separateness and uniqueness, we can be in relationship with each other.

Sometimes churches promote too much enmeshment in relationships. We often fail to keep clear distinctions between God and ourselves. We sometimes confuse our will with the divine will. We speak of the divine with such familiarity that the listener might assume that we have some direct line to the voice of God. When we nurture this perspective, we often set people up to depend on us as their source of divine direction.

In "Leaving Home," for instance, I approach Moses cautiously. Rather than speaking as if from an inside knowledge of what was at issue in Moses' story, I admit that "we do not know what was burning in Moses." I offer that in having "walked with Moses," I found a "maybe" regarding what was happening within the man.

When we encourage codependency in our relationship with God, we imply that people ought to be enmeshed in their relationships with each other. I have seen people "burn out" in service to the church because they did not make distinctions between themselves and the church. They were invested so personally in the church that they could not distinguish what was good for them and what was good for the church. For a relationship to be healthy, clear boundaries must be developed and nurtured. When we know ourselves and remain distinct from the other, we then can explore the gifts that we can give to each other.

They Have Mystery

Healthy relationships are filled with mystery. With the exponential expansion of media during the past twenty years, there has been a shift in culture's expectations regarding mystery. We not only have thousands of hours of television and radio time to fill, but the tingle of anticipation that enhances mystery is also in short supply. Digital communication makes it possible to be in touch with almost anyone at anytime wherever we are. Gone is the space created by writing a letter, putting it in the mail box, waiting for it to arrive, then waiting for the recipient to think about the letter, write a response, and mail it, and then waiting to receive it. Some people expect "instant messaging" and immediate responses. Anticipation is seen as a violation of cultural etiquette. With the exhilaration of communication, the mystery of wonder and anticipation are no longer appreciated.

The presence of television and movies in our culture, along with the Worldwide Web and the Internet, have created a culture that is open to revealing all. Talk shows have no mercy. A celebrity is subject to the exploration of the deepest secrets, with the assumption that nothing is to be hidden. Everything within a person is subject to the light of day, assuming that we will understand and all will be well when that light shines. Mystery is viewed a problem to be solved rather than part of the human condition to be celebrated, loved, feared, hated, teased, rejected and embraced.

This emphasis on the glaring light of revelation has caused us to be suspicious when we do not know everything about another person. Healthy relationships recognize that the other is more than what *we* know and see. It acknowledges that the other person is more than *they* know and see. A healthy relationship is one that has the potential for living and growing because it knows that there is far more within the other and between the other and the self than we can ever possibly see, understand, or know. That is the delight of the divine mystery within creation.

The church must attend to the multiple relationships and help people explore the untapped potential of those relationships. The delight of living is the discovery of more than you knew. It is the surprising awareness of the rich and complex nature of that which God is creating. I have spent a great deal of my life exploring the mind and heart of those within me and those around me. But it is only in the past few years that my life has freed me to explore the depths of body and soul and how complex we each are. Preaching that has potential for contributing to the transforming of life is preaching that acknowledges and celebrates mystery. The "Familiar Strangers" sermon, which you will encounter in the next chapter, invites listeners along on Jacob's journey of wrestling with night and the divine. I seek to give surprising, rich, complex, mysterious things a place in the story of human-divine encounter. Jacob's own dark, dangerous, messy progress invites listeners into deeper and more patient relationship with their own open-ended and mysterious life corners.

They Have Future

Relationships that transform must have a future. When I was single and spent time dating, one of the barriers to developing relationships was the growing awareness on the part of one of the parties that "there is no future in this relationship." There is something within us that not only lives today but imagines our lives tomorrow.

Transformation of people within the community of the church is seldom the result of a few encounters with our ancestors through powerful sermons. Relationships that change who we are have staying power. Evidence can be seen in the response of millions of people to the attacks on the United States on September 11, 2001. The churches, synagogues, and mosques were filled for a few weeks after that date. Fear and anxiety about the future temporarily changed the behavior of many people. But, the renewed relationship with faith communities was temporary. Any long-term change in the way we live our lives in this country was short-lived.

Relationships with power to transform us must wake up the tomorrow in us. They cause us to wonder, plan, calculate, and imagine. They hope that something will happen on the basis of what is happening now. By imagining the future, the moment continues to exist tomorrow. For people to commit themselves to relationships, they need to believe that there will be some important continuing presence that results from the energy they spend getting acquainted with the other.

The church nurtures the sense of future in relationships in its organization and its liturgy. It creates contexts in which people can come together and study, pray, serve, or play. It invites people to participate regularly with others who are pursuing a life of faith. It remembers those who have lived before through memorials and days such as All Saints Day. It keeps alive the memory of those who were a part of the ancient communities and thus helps people who participate in liturgy realize that past relationships continue to be in the future.

They Are Respectful

Healthy relationships reflect respect for the other. Each person is unique. All who have ever lived are different, as are the contexts and histories of their lives. Healthy relationships respect these differences.

The healing quality of healthy relationships is its affirmation of the other. Much of what we remember in the constellation of our soulful and historical relationships is the rejection and pain that came when our uniqueness was not affirmed and respected. Much of what children experience is the rejection of their sense of self as expressed in their emotions and desires. When a child does something that is socially inappropriate, the parent generally calls that action into question. We frequently use shame to help the child learn that she should not act that way if she is to be accepted in this family or culture. For a child in the early stages of development, there is little capacity to distinguish between rejection of what they are doing and a sense of rejection of them as individuals.

For adults to be in healthy relationships, we must show respect for each other as we are. The doubts that plague us grow out of our assessment of reality. When the church listens to our questions and takes seriously the doubts that haunt us, it shows respect for our experience and consequently respect for us. When preaching reflects the awareness that confusion and fear are fundamental to a struggle to live a faithful life—casting Moses as someone who burns, Mary as someone unglued and confused in the dark, and Jacob as someone limping from his night terrors—it helps the listener know that they are respected. To discount our fears and doubts is to discount us.

They Are Honest

Healthy relationships are honest ones. They must have the capacity to speak truth even when the truth is unpleasant. If we can reflect our truth with humility, others will believe us even if they do not agree with us.

The church is sometimes guilty of not speaking truth about the characters they want us to know from the Bible because the truth is sometimes painful. One of my colleagues introduced a group of students to Michal, first wife of David. In her story in 1–2 Samuel, we find a woman who is used, abused, and deceived. She is a pawn between Saul, her father, and David. She also suffers the cruel loss of her five sons from another marriage. This story, when told with honesty and passion, is difficult to hear and painful to imagine. But it is the story of a woman whose presence is important yet often unacknowledged from most of our pulpits. When my colleague told this story to her class, she received an e-mail from a student who was deeply moved to find such an honest story in the Bible—a story that reflected much of what the student had experienced in her life. The honest telling of Michal's story brought forth a painful presence from within the student, but in that pain, the student discovered her own story in the Bible. She came to realize that she was not alone. She opened to the possibility that God might use her words to contribute to a more just and loving future for others. Honesty in relationships has potential healing power.

They Hold Us

When relationships have potential for healing, they hold us as we are. Our healing is enhanced when we find people who can hold our pain and do not try to rescue us from that pain. In a crisis, most of us have increased anxiety that drives us to seek answers, often outside ourselves. But if those answers come from others and do not represent the uniqueness of our own lives, we are deprived of the power that comes from making our own discoveries.

When someone facilitates our meeting persons who have similar questions and anxieties, we can discover in conversation and relationship with them, new ways of being in our situation. When we share with people how we learned to see and discern, we come to our own truth. That truth is not only more valuable in shaping who we are becoming, but it is more empowering. When we develop confidence to discern our own truth in one situation, we develop strength and confidence to do it in other difficult situations.

Jesus illustrates this holding experience in his parables. Parables did not give people answers. They put the listener into different contexts with a story and introduce them to different people who make decisions within the story. But the parable is open ended. Jesus respected the listeners' need and right to discern truth for themselves. That is a witness to his awareness of the uniqueness of each person and his confidence that all people, educated and uneducated alike, have the ability to discover their own truth.

Conclusion

Transformation is the result of being in relationship with people whose presence can bring about change for us. To be in a saving, healing relationship is to become acquainted with people, within us and outside us, whose love, life, honesty, integrity and mystery accompany us and help us discover more life within and around us.

The next chapter of the book explores the multiple contexts in which we preach and what those contexts suggest for how we can preach for healing and hope.

5

The Familiar Strangers

Gen. 32:22–32

First this morning a word of apology–Jesus said, "if a brother or sister has something against you, go and be reconciled before you eat together." During the sermon yesterday, it was pointed out to me by some of you that I represented Mary of Magdalene in a way that was not exactly biblical, that I implied that she was a person of the streets. In no way do I wish to contribute to stereotypes of any persons, and my apologies to Mary and to Mary's community. Our speaker reminded us yesterday that the universal epoch includes honesty, respect, fairness, responsibility, and compassion. In my judgment we owe that not simply to the contemporary community in which we live, but also to the community of saints, to be honest with who they are.

We have begun a journey, a spiritual pilgrimage, as we seek to explore the way the human encounters the Holy and the way the Holy engages in a process of transforming the human. We began with Moses, the one whose burning passion for the oppressed drove him from home; the one whose passion would not be settled by simply sitting still; the one who had a burning heart that would not be eased by taking Tums.

We have listened to and conversed with Mary, who when her home was destroyed, continued to seek the presence of Jesus in the places that she considered sacred, in the presence of sacred memory, who stayed with that memory long enough to hear her name called, long enough for recognition. While Mary was in the garden, she met God in the gardener and was graced by her name being spoken by one who was strangely familiar. If you seek a spiritual pilgrimage, you will leave home, and you will discover those along the way who once were familiar; those who may have become strangers to you. But on that pilgrimage you will also come across people you have never known, and according to our heritage, we are to welcome the stranger because the stranger may be a messenger from the Divine. Strangers are those who teach us something about ourselves that we may not know.

When I began this particular part of the pilgrimage of my life, I enjoyed going among strangers. I enjoyed traveling to new places. One day I got an e-mail from the dean of the seminary. He sent an e-mail to the faculty and asked, "Would any one of you be able to leave in three weeks and go to Fiji to represent this school at an international meeting?" I thought for about three seconds and responded, "I'll go." I had an advantage over many of my colleagues because I was on a pilgrimage. I was not burdened with a lot of the responsibilities that those who had been around the seminary for a while had, and my family was not in need of my presence. I was free to travel.

I was in a meeting once where a novelist made this statement, "When we are writing novels, we frequently go among strangers, because it is said we discover who *we* are among strangers." The pilgrimage of faith is one where we meet many a stranger on this road of reluctant pilgrims, strangers who teach us about ourselves.

But it is not easy to welcome strangers, for frequently we feel that they might be enemies. They might threaten our self-understanding. When we are out in strange places, it is very difficult for us to feel secure enough to engage the stranger.

When we are outside of the ritual safety of our own space, we become nervous about those people who are different from us.

When I was traveling in Vietnam and Cambodia in the mid-eighties on a peace mission for the church, I remember getting on an airplane. I had been on many airplanes in my life—but I remember getting on an airplane in Hanoi to fly to Phnom Penh, Cambodia. As we boarded we filled all the seats. Then I saw people putting chicken crates in the isle and sitting on them. Some of the crates had live chickens in them. I sat down and was a little nervous because people had not buckled their seat belts. I waited for the announcement, "Please pay attention to the flight attendant while she demonstrates how to buckle your seat…" an announcement I had heard many times and mostly ignored. But I wanted that announcement. I wanted the security of the familiar. Well, the announcement never came. And no one told us to put "our seat backs forward and our tray tables up." No one told us to where the oxygen masks were and how they would drop down but not inflate. No one said, "If you are traveling with a small child, put your mask on first before you assist the child." I was really nervous. I missed the ritual. The rituals, even when I ignore them, help me feel secure. This is the way you fly. This is familiar. The ritual creates home in an airplane, and this airplane was not home.

We get nervous among strangers, and often we close down. Often when we feel threatened, when we are outside of our realm of safety, we feel threatened by these people and begin to push them away. I have been struck by many of the feelings I have heard from people after the World Trade Center collapsed and the Pentagon was penetrated. I hear people say, "We must separate from those people who are different. We have to protect ourselves from those people who are different."

We are frightened people because that which we have trusted has been violated, and now all who look different feel to us as if they might be threatening enemies. I listen to that, and then I remember Jesus, who said, "Love your enemies" (Mt. 5:44) because it is the stranger who may even be your enemy who teaches you who you are. To be on a pilgrimage is to be among strangers.

You remember Jacob? He was on a pilgrimage. He was on a pilgrimage to visit his brother, the stranger, the one whom he had not seen for years, the one whom he had violated. He was going to a sacred place, a sacred memory: to the memory of his family. He was going to meet his brother in a place of terror and hope and love and longing, a brother who was a stranger.

And on his way he encountered another stranger. Left alone across the river from his family, he met a stranger in the night. (I am struck by how many times these messages from God come to people in the night, in the dark.) He encountered a stranger in the dark, a stranger with whom he contended. I'm convinced that to discover the Divine in the pilgrimage of life, one must spend a good bit of time wrestling in the dark. These wrestling matches of our lives come to us in spaces where we cannot see clearly the stranger with whom we struggle.

We do not know our fears. We cannot name why it is we are unsettled or feel frightened. Somehow it is dark around us, and much of the struggle of the pilgrimage of the soul is in the dark. It is in the dark with those people, those characters of our own soul whom we do not know.

Jacob wrestled with a stranger, someone he did not know. Jacob did not run from this stranger. Jacob did not try to hide behind some fortress to protect himself from this night terror. He wrestled with it. He engaged it. The stranger even wanted to run from Jacob, and Jacob said, "No! Do not leave me until you bless me!" (Gen. 3:26)

Is there a word to those of us who wake up at two in the morning and cannot go back to sleep? Are we like Jacob being given the gift of the strangers with whom we can struggle—strangers who will not let us go, strangers we will not let go until we are blessed? I know many who believe that night struggles are counterproductive. I tried to tell myself, in the nights of my life, that it is counterproductive to keep obsessing about something. But sometimes obsessions are the sacred that simply is too powerful until it is wrestled to the ground.

We are told that Jacob wrestled with this dark night until he was blessed. There are people who will tell you to "just get over it," who will turn on the light when you are sitting in the dark. They say, "See, isn't this an incredible world? Quit sitting in the dark." There are people who will tell you, "Give up your passion for painting. Give up your desire to dance. Give up that drive to sing to the heavens. Give it up!" But you keep hanging on and wrestling because it is the passion of your life—hanging on until it blesses you. Do not let anyone convince you and try to force you into the light when you are still wrestling in the night. When you try to come into the light too soon, it looks fake. It is like the watching wrestling on television. There is nothing but the fantasy.

What is it to be blessed by the stranger? Elie Wiesel in his book *The Forgotten* has one of the characters ask, "Tell me about yourself," to which he responds, "I'm like a book. I cannot read myself. You will have to read me." Strangers read us and help us see ourselves. They bless us, not by our getting acquainted with them but by their helping us get acquainted with ourselves.

Jacob wrestled with this dark night and said, "Tell me who you are." The stranger said, "Why do you want to know?" Many times we think our spiritual journeys are pilgrimages for the purpose of finding out who God is, so we can access God on our time. But to wrestle with the Divine is not to find and domesticate God. To wrestle with the Divine is to learn who we are, to learn our new name.

The stranger asked Jacob, "What's your name?" He said, "I'm Jacob." "No longer are you Jacob. Once you've been wrestling with God, you have a new name, and the new name for you is Israel, the one who strives with God and prevails," the stranger said. The pilgrimage of faith is the wrestling with God until you get a new name, a new identity, a new passport, and a new self-understanding.

But do not expect that you will leave that encounter dancing. In his wrestling, Jacob was struck in the hip, and he went away limping. To encounter the Holy is to be scarred for life with a new identity and a new limp. Your friends will know something has happened to you. You will be wounded. You will limp. But on the pilgrimage of faith there is a whole community of limpers out there who are trying to walk carefully into their new name, and it is in that community that we are sustained on this continuing pilgrimage toward home.

6

The Contexts for Preaching Healing

When we stand in the pulpit to preach, we look into the faces of people who are formed by multiple contexts. They walk into the sanctuary from the context of a political and social world, a world of family and work, school and farm, constancy and change, loss and gain, conflict and compassion, and despair and hope. To preach in a way that will allow persons to be in touch *with* and touched *by* relationships that can bring healing and hope requires careful attention to the multiple contexts that shape them.

Shrinking World

One of the characteristics of our current context is that we live in a shrinking world. I was standing in the post office near my home in Indianapolis. It was the week before Christmas, and we procrastinators were waiting in line. As I sought to calm my impatience, I became aware of the din of conversation. I looked around, and there were seventeen people. Four were Hispanics, three of Middle Eastern origin, two from Asia, four African Americans, and four of European descent. A mini-United Nations gathered less than a mile from my home.

As I think about the changing context in which we are called to preach, I am conscious of the shrinking world. The diversity of those who make up our towns and cities is increasing. The complexity of living in a culturally multifaceted world isn't the exclusive concern of those involved in international politics, but it is becoming an issue impacting virtually every local community in the United States. The presence of this diversity is not a new reality for most urban areas of our country. Immigrants have governed this country for most of its history, since Europeans invaded these shores over four hundred years ago. Urban areas have always lived with the complexity of cultural diversity.

But this diversity is also becoming characteristic of much of the rest of the country. As the agonizingly slow evolution of empowerment of African Americans in the North and the South develops, many rural communities struggle to find ways of living with diversity, of honoring the differences while affirming similarities. As people of African descent claim their heritage and assert its rightful place on this continent, the culture works to become inclusive of divergent perspectives.

This shrinking world is being experienced even where there was once cultural hegemony. When I grew up in a small town in southern Missouri, there were no persons of color among the 5000 people who lived there. This was not by accident. This was by the design of those in power. When I returned for a class reunion a few years ago, I discovered that Hispanics now make up 11 percent of the population. Even communities that were insular in the past are experiencing the cultural diversity that characterizes the context in which we preach.

We not only preach in the context of a shrinking world. It is also that of the illusion of a shrinking world. Most of us have more encounters with persons of different cultures than we did forty years ago. But one of the characteristics of the context in which we preach is the illusion of intimacy and community. This illusion must be faced when we preach.

The increased methods of communication have made people *feel* that they are connected when they are really not. Television and the Internet give us the impression that we are a community when we are not really. Talk shows make us feel that there is some intimacy between the people on the television and us. We feel connected to the victims of the hurricanes, the victims of rape and robbery, and the celebrities convicted of crimes.

But we do not form real community. We are not living where the consequences of our relationships with them have a real impact on how we live our lives. To feel anger or pain when we watch someone weep over the loss of her son to a drive-by shooting in another city makes us feel that we are connected. But we are not called to respond as if the mother lived next door and the son grew up with our daughter. They are not really us—there is just the illusion that they are.

The increased sources of information also give us the illusion that we are experiencing a shrinking world. When we read about persons who are suffering in Iraq or Afghanistan, we have a sense that we know who they are and what they are going through. And to the extent that we have empathy and can gain some insights into them through the words of others reporting on them, we are in relationship with them. But it is an illusion to believe that we are in community simply because we know something about people.

This confusing reality is a part of the context in which the gospel is preached and heard. We not only have to preach where the lives of persons in our community are intertwined with the lives of persons who speak different languages and reflect different values, but we have to preach where people are manipulated by illusions of intimacy. We not only have to preach in a way that contributes to the listener's ability to negotiate the real lives that they touch each day, but we have to preach to those who feel they are connected to these disembodied persons they meet on the Internet or television.

When we preach to facilitate healing relationships, it is important to help people identify and develop *real* relationships. Only real relationships have transforming power. When Jacob wrestles with the stranger in "Familiar Strangers," (chapter 5) I introduce Jacob and the stranger-in-whom-the-divine-comes only after couching them in the context of a post-September 11 United States. My hope is that the listeners have experienced the terror and the vulnerability of a home that is not safe, assumptions about life as it is that are open to attack by unexpected and unknown persons. I then try to introduce the

"Other" not as someone over there to be nice to or "do unto," but as someone close enough to wrestle with and be attacked by, someone close enough to touch with both blessing and curse.

Cultural Shifts

Subtle forces of cultural change are another contextual reality that helps shape the way persons listen to sermons. Culture is like our skin. It is something that helps define who we are, but it is seldom something that we pay attention to. It is so much a part of who we know ourselves to be that we do not even realize its influence on us.

We can look at our cultural reality in a variety of ways. Jennifer Michael Hecht, in *Doubt: A History*,[1] explores history from the angle of the periods of doubt. She believes that history is normally written in times of stability and constancy. But she also believes that following each such period of intellectual history, were periods of chaos and doubt. She suggests that those times of chaos produced the great innovations that were developed and celebrated in stable times.

I believe that when we use this template to understand our cultural context, we are in a period of more doubt and confusion than stability and certainty. Many businesses find themselves unable to compete in a shrinking world in which the old values do not seem to apply. People often feel anxiety because the certainty they had about their own values are challenged by their relationship with the values of their teen-aged children. The confusion and chaos that these families feel because of the shifting cultural values causes great distress.

When we preach a sermon, many of the people who are listening often are sitting in a pool of chaos and doubt. They are anxious and fearful because they do not know what to believe or how to live. The overwhelming influx of information and stimuli keeps persons off balance and wondering what really matters. They feel nothing is secure, much less sacred. They are a people who can resonate with a Jacob whose night-terror wrestling leaves him limping in the morning.

Another way of looking at the current cultural context is "postmodern." This describes the end of an era without any clear understanding of the emerging one. Richard Hamm, former President and General Minister of the Christian Church (Disciples of Christ) in the United States and Canada, believes that the modern era in Western civilization began in the early-fifteenth century and ended in the mid-twentieth century. He indicates that modern-era Western thought and culture were characterized universally by immutable physical laws; linear, rational, symmetrical thinking; the building blocks of the world order were nation-states. Authority was granted by office and was hierarchical; a broad social consensus was dominated and controlled by white Anglo-Saxon males; communication was oratorical, formal and indirect; and progress was inevitable.

Hamm calls the current context "postmodern," one in which the universe is characterized by relativity. In it thinking is non-linear and asymmetrical with many centers of focus. The building blocks are not only nation-states, but also mass communications and the market. Authority is granted by relationships, and this diversity of power means that there are diverse and varied voices shaping our world. Communication is conversational, direct, and informal, and progress is not inevitable but possible.[2]

This analysis of the context leads the preacher to the awareness that if one must speak, it is important to speak with humility. Some may feel the impulse to lament the end of an era or try to challenge the postmodern era by attempting to reconstruct the modern era. But knowing that the modern era is over and that there is a new age emerging can open the preacher to consider communicating differently. My intention is to show how preaching to facilitate healing relationships is a way of being heard that is consistent with the postmodern sensibilities.

The emerging postmodern era is grounded in what some call the New Science. Margaret Wheatley, in *Leadership and the New Science*,[3] believes that the replacement of Newtonian physics with quantum physics as the primary way the world is understood has caused us to view life through new lenses.

> Each of us lives and works in organizations designed from Newtonian images of the universe. We manage by separating things into parts; we believe that influence occurs as a direct result of force exerted from one person to another; we engage in complex planning for

a world that we keep expecting to be predicable, and we search continually for better methods of objectively perceiving the world.[4]

This way of perceiving the world necessarily causes the preacher to look at preaching as an attempt to impact the thinking of the listeners. The hope is that they might work hard to plan the outcomes they desire by their acting in a given situation. Our sermons attempt to analyze by taking things apart and seeing how they work, so that the listener might understand and then change themselves and their world.

But when we understand the world from the perspective of quantum physics, we preach differently. Wheatley says that the new science operates on the assumption that organizations (and I would say individuals who are whole systems in themselves) cannot be changed simply by

> "[I]mposing a model developed elsewhere. So little transfers to, or even inspires, those trying to work in their own organizations. [Also] the new physics cogently explains that there is no objective reality out there waiting to reveal its secrets. There are no recipes or formulae, no checklists or advice that describes 'reality'. There is only what we create through our engagement with others and with events. Nothing really transfers; everything is always new and different and unique to each of us."[5]

In quantum physics, "*relationship* is the key determiner of what is observed and how particles manifest themselves. Particles come into being and are observed only in relationship to something else. They do not exist as independent 'things'. These unseen *connections* between what were previously thought to be separate entities are the fundamental element of creation."[6]

This understanding of the nature of existence creates a much more fluid and unpredictable context for preaching. It assumes that the act of facilitating relationship is an act of creation. What exists is a result of particles or people in relationship with other particles and people. For a preacher to contribute to a re-creative energy, the preacher must work to help divergent people come into relationship with each other.

If we look at people living in this new world as people struggling with doubt and surrounded by an understanding of the world as unstable and unpredictable, we can explore preaching from a new perspective. The language I find most helpful to describe the context in which we live is proposed by Zygmunt Bauman in *Liquid Modernity*.[7] He suggests that the times are most characterized as "liquid." He quotes Paul Valery:

> "Interruptions, incoherence, surprise are the ordinary conditions of our life. They have even become real needs for people, whose minds are no longer fed… by anything that lasts. We no longer know how to make boredom bear fruit." He continues, "It is now the smaller, the lighter, the portable that signifies improvement and 'progress.' Traveling light, rather than holding on tightly to things deemed attractive for their reliability and solidity—that is, for their heavy weight, substantiality and unyielding power of resistance—is now the asset of power."[8]

For preaching to be effective in this context, we must take this fluid nature of things into account. In a day when we believed that matter was fixed and that we could nail truth down the way we could secure a building, it might have been appropriate to preach doctrine and dogma. But in a time when change is constant and people do not even have sand on which to build their house (much less a rock), preaching must reflect what people have to work with. We humans are in a constant state of flux, changing and growing, making new and unpredictable discoveries as we experience fresh relationships. Preaching must attend to this liquid time if it is to assist people to live faithfully before the creative God who is constantly doing new things. It must facilitate people's relationship with living reality so that there is confidence and courage for living.

When Deborah and I were on our honeymoon, we discovered the power of relationship in liquid time. We both were snorkeling in the crystal clear waters off St. John in the Virgin Islands. The fish were bright blues and yellows. But I was having trouble. I kept sucking air into my mask. I would get it cleared out, go under again seeking to float and examine the beauty before my eyes. But water would invade the mask again. Finally Deborah, who was more experienced in the water than I, asked "Are you afraid?" Being unwilling to admit fear or unable to know my own feelings, I said, "No, I'm not afraid. I can swim." But, after several attempts to keep my mask clear, I admitted, "I might be a little nervous." She said, "Give me your hand." And so we floated around for a couple of minutes as I held her hand. My anxiety eased and within a few minutes, I relaxed and from then on could enjoy the world around me.

In liquid times, we need to be in relationships with people who can hold our hand and ease our anxiety. We need the courage that comes from knowing that we are not alone, that we have companions for our journey. Preaching that facilitates these relationships will empower people with courage and confidence to live abundant lives into the future.

As we explore preaching as the art of facilitating healing relationships we will assume these understandings of the context.

Personal Contexts

The way people experience their lives shapes how they hear the words of the preacher. Some people live in a constant state of change; they are in continual transition. William Bridges, in *Transitions: Making Sense of Life's Changes,* explores the anatomy of a transition and indicates that all transitions begin with an ending.[9] Every change results in something ending. The world is never the same when something changes. This requires that people attend to the losses that occur when something ends. It is necessary that people grieve losses so that they can move toward the new life and world that is out ahead of them.[10] When we preach to people who are living in a state of constant transition, it is important for us to attend to the grieving process, helping people learn to live in the absence of what has disappeared.

In his analysis of transitions, Bridges reveals that an ending is followed by a neutral zone. This is a space created by the collapse of certain structures that sustain, form, and give identity to the person. He calls this a time of pure energy. It is energy that has little form to contain it. In the biblical motif, this is a time of wilderness or desert. It is a time when there are few signposts that give clear direction. It is a time of fear and exhilaration, of creativity and terror. When we preach with awareness of the changes within and around listeners during wilderness times in their lives, this helps shape how we communicate. We must attend to the anxiety and confusion that is in the heart and soul of the persons in the pew.

A transition ends when there is a new beginning. New beginnings are times when new energy and clarity for the future converge, and there is new form, new life. These are not easy times. New beginnings, like birth, are painful and messy. But they are the occasion for celebration and achievement. Like wilderness experiences in the Bible, they are often times when not all will cross over the river to the promised land. Some might not be able to make the shift from wilderness wandering to community building. The effective preacher who is speaking to people in this part of the transition needs to attend to the fallout that comes from new beginnings. And she needs to be ready to deal with the loss that comes from an ending. This is what is like to live in a context of continual cultural change. The preacher is constantly dealing with persons who are going through transitions.

But the preacher is not simply dealing with the transitions of individual members of the congregation; she is preaching to a congregation that is also going through transitions. The congregation is experiencing constant change that results from new people coming into the community. The changes that occur in the neighborhood and the city create transitions for congregations. The city's changes may result in the ending of some access to some of its resources. If the city has had an economic base in manufacturing and that work is redistributed to communities in other parts of the country or world, the city will suffer major change. The economic activities on which they have depended will end. There will be anxiety and fear in that ending, the fear and terror of wilderness. We will not know where our next meal is coming from. The city will be haunted by uncertainty. When that happens, the congregation will find itself in a wilderness of unknowing as well. And when a city or neighborhood gets something new, the congregation will have to adjust to that as well. If younger families move into the neighborhood and their values do not include worship in congregations on Sunday morning, but instead require them to be on the soccer field, the new beginning for the neighborhood will require adjustment on the part of the congregation.

To help a congregation deal with these cultural shifts, the preacher will contribute to a more positive outcome if she helps the congregation grieve their losses, helping them to welcome the new strangers into their world. The ability to relearn our world after change and loss requires the capacity to name the losses, feel the pain, express anger, remember the past as it really was, share the guilt for not achieving what had been desired, forgive the self and the past for not being all we wanted it to be, express gratitude for the good that has been our life, play with new ideas, practice a new life and then experience a new birth.[11] If preaching is going to be effective, it must attend to the issues of change and find ways to help people explore ways of being faithful in the emerging culture.

Liturgical Context

One of the most important ways of attending to the cultural and personal contexts of the listeners is to understand how the sermon nests within the liturgy of the congregation. Liturgy is the work of the people who gather before God to worship. It is that which structures the experience of the participant and gives shape and form to the activity of public praise.

Different churches have different emphasis within their liturgies. I am part of the left wing of the Reformation, and the liturgy of my church was focused on word. I grew up believing strongly in reason's ability to organize and understand reality. My faith had been deeply rational and I was not very tolerant of words that did not make sense to my rational mind.

But I reached a time when words became ashes in my mouth. My first wife had been diagnosed with a rare cancer. I was on a three-month sabbatical from my congregation. As I traveled to various cities for continuing education events, I found myself drawn to worship at Episcopal churches. Whereas my own church focused on the word, Episcopal churches seemed to focus on worship. Whereas many in my church try to make the liturgy and the sermon relevant and contingent, the Episcopal churches seemed to focus on the familiar. God was present in the ancient liturgical practice of song, prayer, Eucharist, and scripture reading. They did not seem particularly interested in whether it made sense to me or if I was happy. They had a ritual practice that was predictable, and the worship was pretty much the same whether I was in Philadelphia or Denver. At that point in my life, I did not want people to pay attention to me. I wanted to be held in a service that recited familiar phrases from the centuries.

I discovered healing by being present to the saints through the tradition. I discovered grace by people not focusing on my personal life situation. I discovered what Belden Lane describes in *The Solace of Fierce Landscapes: Exploring Desert and Mountain Spirituality*.[12] He discovered healing for his pain over his mother's death by being in the fierce landscapes of the western United States. He discovered grace when he was in the presence of that which ignored him. I discovered comfort and peace by being in the presence of a liturgy that was ancient and familiar even as it ignored my personal situation.

I spent several years wondering why I was attracted to the ancient liturgy of the Episcopal church. Then after the multiple and intense losses that followed, I made a discovery in one of the most of unlikely places—a bookstore. I had spent most of my adult life reading and collecting books. I loved books. Books line all the walls of my office. They are friends: old friends whose presence on the shelves reminds me of who I am by reflecting where I came from; and new friends who hint at where I might be going.

But at the point of significant loss in my life when my soul was in chaos, books turned on me. They did not provide comfort, but rather created nausea. I had made sacred pilgrimages to bookstores when I went to different cities, but I suddenly found that I could not even enter a bookstore without feeling sick to my stomach. I was developing an unconscious understanding that God is silence, not word. Bookstores had just too many empty words screaming out at me from the bookshelves.

But I found that I had to visit bookstores from time to time just to keep doing the work I was doing or get a gift for someone else. It was Saturday morning, and I was in a megabookstore.

I went to the children's section to get a birthday present for one of my granddaughters. I asked the clerk for the book and while she was searching for it, I saw parents sitting in bright plastic beanbag chairs holding children on their laps. They were reading stories to them. It was then that I realized that this picture of parents and children and books was a model for the way liturgy and preaching work within congregations.

The children can sit safely on the lap of the parent and feel the security of the parent's arms holding them. They feel the mother's heartbeat against their back. In this place the parent can read the child stories about wolves and witches, and the child can face their fears. They can face their fears in the lap of security and safety. They can feel their heartbeat increase as they hear of the chase and they can feel themselves drawn to courage while feeling safe in their parents' arms.

Liturgy is like the lap of the parent. It holds the listener in a safe and secure setting while the preacher introduces them to the strange and scary world of what it is to be a person of faith who serves the God of the Hebrew people and the God of Jesus Christ. The human heart's desire to grow requires both safety and adventure. The liturgy provides the safety while the preaching provides the adventure. In the safety of the familiar, the preacher can introduce the stranger.

I discovered that the word of the prophet that challenges and calls us out beyond ourselves is more likely entertained with possibility if it is spoken within a context that feels safe. Preaching within the security of a familiar liturgy helps people face their fears and discover courage as they seek to live faithfully in the world.

The liturgy is the practice of what the community knows itself to be. The liturgy is enfleshed self-awareness. What the people do in worship reflects what they know themselves to be.

In *On Liturgical Theology* [13] Aidan Kavanagh outlines the fundamental structure of medieval worship, fundamentally the form that most Christian communities still practice. He suggests that this form facilitates the weekly practice of what it is to live the Christian life. It reflects the character of the Christian spirit. [14]

Christians begin worship by *gathering*. The churches in Europe would begin their service early in the morning, headed by priests singing as they walked through the streets, collecting people from the whole city, and leading them toward the church. Christians are people who gather with all creation. They are people who gather with rich and poor, sick and healthy, young and old, stranger and friend. All creation gathers to worship the creator. With this paradigm, Christians quickly learn that they are part of creation. When the people gathered and confessed their sins, they leveled the community. All are sinners, and all receive words of assurance of forgiveness, thus becoming part of the whole creation who is of God and who is forgiven by God. They become one people who are forgiven.

The second thing that Christians do when we worship is to *listen* for God's word. We listen to scripture and sermon, song and prayer. We listen for an insight from the divine that might illumine the meaning of our lives as part of this whole of creation.

This is practicing what it is to be Christian in the world. We gather with strangers with whom we are one, and we listen for the divine within creation. The practice of listening developed in worship is exercised in the daily life of the world. God who creates all is present and speaks through the daily living and loving of our lives. We pay attention to the world and we love the world, trusting and believing that the divine will be revealed, not only in the human creation around us, but in the whole of creation.

Listening in worship is practicing the art of listening humans into life. We know who we are by how we word our world. We know we are people of Moses and Jesus by the way we word our stories, which define what we value. When we as Christians are unleashed on the world with ears open to listening for the divine in the lives of those around us, we create a space in which people might speak themselves into divine awareness. The art of listening people into good news is such an important part of our world, which is primarily interested in speaking to others about what is available for purchase. It is a refreshing gift to the world for people to wander it with ears open to the divine that is within all that is created.

The third component of Christian worship is making offering. After we gather with strangers, we become one with them in confession, forgiveness, and listening for divine insight. We then make ourselves an offering to God. We bring the gifts of the earth in bread and wine and offer them to God that the divine might take them, making them a blessing for all. We bring our money and time, given to the mission of divine love that these broken gifts might be combined with the gifts of others and with divine grace. We make a gift of redemption for the earth.

This liturgical practice becomes a weekly model for the way we make ourselves a blessing for the earth. We bring our broken and inadequate selves and give ourselves to the healing of the world. We are not called in worship to heal the earth. We are called to make who we are as an offering to the one who brings redemption. In our lifetime, we will see little progress toward the completion of the reign of God. But by worship, we affirm that we believe that it is in the giving of these broken pieces of our lives that the divine uses us for the healing of creation.

After we have gathered with strangers and listened for the divine word and made ourselves an offering to God, we then *depart in peace.* Christians gather to practice spiritual virtues and then leave to be leaven for the earth. We do not gather in the name of Christ simply to find healing for ourselves, but we gather for the purpose of leaving. We gather not for the sake of the church, but for the sake of the world that is loved by God.

People of the Christian faith come into relationships in the Christian community to be transformed from isolated and fragmented persons to persons who give themselves with courage to the world. We are sustained by the relationships we have with our ancestors through the liturgy, challenged by the relationships we have with our ancestors through the scriptures.

Preaching that facilitates healing relationships is done within these contexts: a rapidly changing world, hearts and souls in constant transitions, and held in the lap of grace by the liturgy. In the next section of this book, we explore how these concepts of transformation through relationships shape the development, writing, and preaching of a sermon.

7

The Reluctant Pilgrim Sermon

Sounds of Silence

1 Kings 9:11–18

The pilgrimage moves on. With Moses, we experienced the burning longing of desire created by the loss of privilege and the exposure to the larger world, to the suffering of those who were oppressed. With Mary, we experienced the hot tears that come when one's home disappears while we wait to be recognized by the Divine. And with Jacob, we have wrestled on that road, wrestled with the dark demons of fear, wrestling long enough to have those that appear to be evil give us a new name.

The journey is often long and grueling. To be on the road is exhausting. It is hard to be constantly adapting to environments that are new and changing. Sometimes we become so exhausted that we cannot speak. Sometimes we become so limp that we cannot sing, and all we can do is sit. Sometimes it is negotiating the new roads of life that come to us not by our own choice but by the choice of life itself, negotiating the losses that come because we have loved and because that love has disappeared. But sometimes it is also exhaustion that comes from the loss of a dream, a dream that has been achieved, because a dream achieved is no longer a dream.

She worked for several years on her dissertation. She studied, researched, wrote, talked to her professors, went back and rewrote, and rewrote, and finally, finally she finished her dissertation. She walked across the stage and received her diploma. She sunk into a major depression, for she was lost. She did not know what to do because her dream had been achieved and she was exhausted.

Elijah had been successful, and one of the most dangerous things in life is to be successful. Elijah had achieved what no one else could achieve. Elijah had struggled with the gods of the culture, had struggled and invited his own God to come and to transform the culture. And to his surprise, God had come. God had come, and Elijah had achieved his dream. And then he was depressed. He sat down under a broom tree and complained to God.

We exhaust ourselves, and when we do, whether it is because our world has changed *against* our will or because it has changed *by* our will, we become exhausted, and our body slows us down sometimes. Sometimes we get sick. I remember my dad, who worked hard to raise five children in a time in which there were very few resources available. He worked hard day and night. He built three Dairy Queens, and he was responsible for managing from eight in the morning until eleven at night. And I remember those few vacations we took. They began with a migraine headache. When my exhausted father let down and sought to relax, his body's stress accumulated in his head and created pain. He had to stop. The body shuts us down sometimes when we are exhausted, and we have to slow down. We have to find a space to slow the pace so that strength can be restored.

In my journey, the car was the place that became my sanctuary because I could get out of the city and on the road. One of my discoveries was that I no longer wanted to drive the highways. Interstates annoyed me. I started driving the back roads, even from my house to the church. I would drive through the neighborhoods. No highways. I drove from city to city on the blue highways. I went through towns that had wilted with the heat of an economic collapse. These were back roads where I could still see those Mobil horses on gasoline signs. I saw faded signs on the side of barns that said, "Bare Alignment." I saw sad-eyed five-and-dime stores staring at me as I drove by. That was where I wanted to be. I wanted to be slow.

The highway annoyed me. I did not understand that until I was reading a novel by Milan Kundera called *Immortality*.[1] He said, "The road is a strip of ground over which one walks. A highway is different from a road, because it is merely a line that connects one point with another. A highway has meaning only in that it gets you from one place to another. A road celebrates the space along the way." And then he said, "Before roads and paths disappeared from the landscape, they disappeared from the human soul."[2] And I realized that in my own exhaustion, I was seduced by the back roads, not only of the countryside but the back roads of my soul, the roads where space is valued, the roads that are not simply points that connect one desire with another, but spaces that celebrate life along the way. I was tired of highways, where I missed my life. I wanted to notice and live my life slow.

Some back roads—as one author who writes about Vermont has said—are dirt roads that blend into the environment. "The back roads and the dirt roads police themselves. They have their own speed bumps. You can't go fast."[3] Deborah and I were recently driving in California. We looked at the map and followed the scenic highway. It took much longer to get where we were going because of all the switchbacks and the stop signs, but we saw twice as much because we had to drive more slowly. When we slow down, we discover the gift of life that is available, not simply from point A to point B but the gift of life that is available along the way.

Annie Dillard, in that incredible book *Pilgrim at Tinker Creek*,[4] has slowed down so much that she has seen the incredible workings of the Divine mystery in the minutest characters. She talks about a group of experimenters who studied one single grass plant, a grass plant of winter rye grown in a greenhouse for four months and taken apart from the soil and looked at. Underneath the microscope, they counted the root hairs. (One *does* have to wonder what provokes such behavior). During the four months the plant had grown it had set forth almost four hundred miles of root. One plant, four hundred miles! That is about three miles a day. In this one grass plant were fourteen million distinct roots. Now Ms. Dillard observes that this is mighty impressive, but when they got down to the root hairs, it boggles the mind completely. In those same four months, the rye plant created fourteen billion–that is a "b"–fourteen billion root hairs, and those little strands, tied end to end, reached six thousand miles.[5]

Maybe slowing down enough to count root hairs is not a bad discipline for those who need to attend to their own soul. It is amazing what you can discover if you just slow down and dig in and listen to the minutest sound within the soul.

Sometimes it is not enough to slow down. Sometimes we simply have to stop. Sometimes we have to find that sanctuary space to silence the sounds around us, so that the sounds of silence might sing to us. Sometimes we have to find a cave. Elijah had to find a cave to settle the noise, the noise of the wind and the noise of the earthquake. You have to overcome the noise of the television, the noise of the Internet, and the noise of fire burning, burning the soul. You have to settle down into the darkness of a cave somewhere and silence the sounds, so that the sounds of silence might sing a new life.

In my journey I have discovered the gift of silence, a space of healing, a space in which I could be at rest and not be stimulated by the overwhelming demands of the world. But when I went into the cave of silence, I discovered how frightening the emptiness can be when all those words that once filled my life were not around me. I felt abandoned by God, although there were those around me who suggested that maybe I had abandoned God rather than God abandoning me. But whatever the case, this is not a matter of making judgments about who is at fault. It is simply a naming of the experience of emptiness, of absence.

For years I wondered where God was, and then it came to me. Then it came to me that God is the emptiness. God is that empty space. I was looking for the God who makes sounds. I was looking for the God who filled me with spirit, but I discovered that God also comes by creating empty space. God becomes that empty space within, ready to reach out and receive the creation of God anew. Sometimes our longing for the God that we have known blinds us to the God who is yet to be revealed. To go into that empty space is to go into a space where one can hear anew the music of the soul.

This morning I listened to the Motet Choir. You did not know it, but the last three days, one of my ears has been stopped up. But today, I could hear out of both ears. When you can hear the sopranos and the altos, as well as the tenors and basses, it is so much more beautiful. And I could hear all the pipes in the organ, not just half of them. To go into the cave is to unstop the other half of your head, so that you can hear in stereophonic sound.

One of the ways that I have tried to understand that in my own journey is to consider that there is a chorus of our lives, the songs of our lives to which we dance. They are songs that are in four-part harmony. There is the part that, when it is sung, reminds us of our past. It is the rich tradition of our common memory. It is the stories of our families. It is the stories of our faith . It is the stories of our nation and the heroes of our nation. It is the stories of the saints of old. There is one whole line in the music of the soul that sings those stories and that shapes how we act and how we live.

There is another part of the soul's music that is the sounds and the words of the contemporary communities in which we live. There are those who are around us, our family right here and now, the friends around us who speak to us, the culture, the voices from Asia, the voices from Afghanistan, the voices from Pakistan, and the voices from Northern Ireland. These are voices from our contemporary world that shape us, and they are a whole line of the music to which our soul listens.

Then there are those voices from deep within, those bass voices of the soul, those voices that are so deep and so embedded in the bone marrow that we simply do not know where they came from. They simply function as our conscience. They are the voices that cause us to have a visceral response to what happens around us. They are those voices deep and base within us.

And then there are soprano voices from the future, calling us into that which we have yet to discover and know, those voices that whisper us into a future and invite us to certain spaces, certain actions tomorrow, and the next day, and the next year. And in order to be whole spiritual persons, it requires listening to all of the voices, and discerning the melody, and discerning the parts until it becomes a song that sings us into our future.

But we must become silent for a while to hear that song because some of those parts are only whispered. Some of those parts cannot be heard with the sounds that surround. It is in the cave that those whispered voices have a chance to emerge, and to find their own voice, and to bloom.

A few years ago, I was driving up the coast of California and Oregon, camping my way, sleeping on the beach, staring at the stars. When I got into Washington, the coastal road disappeared and I moved inland. I headed on north and saw a sign, "Mt. St. Helen." I had to go see. And the closer I got to that wounded mountain, the more at home I felt. The evergreens turned to gray ash. The ground was barren and moonlike. I went to the visitors' center, and I began to read what that was like on the day the earth exploded and the side blew out of the mountain. I began to read about how the lava had simply vaporized the landscape, how it had vandalized the valleys, and how the water and the lakes had simply been washed out. New lakes were created, and old lakes disappeared. The place had simply disappeared under the gray ash of loss and destruction.

But I noticed an amazing thing when I slowed down. Some yellow flowers were beginning to sprout out of stumps. There were plants beginning to bloom, and there were little animals on the ground. And I read that the only thing that survived were the seeds and the animals that were underground.

When we are driven into caves of our lives and struck speechless, we are often driven into the underground where there is life waiting to be born, where there is new life waiting to bloom. And all of a sudden that which at one point felt like a tomb becomes the womb of new life.

8

Introducing People in
the Beginning of the Sermon

Since we are changed or transformed by relationships, the sermons that have the potential for inviting change are those that facilitate relationships. To preach in this way enables people to live more fully by being in relationships to those who can help heal their brokenness. People desire relationships so that they are not alone.

I was recently sitting in the airport people watching. I was struck by a vision of everyone being in relationship. Even those who were alone were in relationship. People were on cell phones making contact with other people by voice or answering machine. Others were reading the morning paper or digesting a book or magazine. Others were watching a movie on their iPods. Others were text-messaging. Others were sending e-mails. Everyone seemed to be in relationship to someone else. They were all speaking or listening to the voices of others.

But in the midst of the cacophonous chaos of multiple voices, I think we long to meet people who can help us know who we are and how we might live more deeply and fully. We long for an oral family album with picture stories about people who give us a sense of identity. We want to get to know some people who can help us find some center to our lives and discover some meaning and purpose for our existence.

And those of us who preach know that it is through the presence of others that people not only find friendship and love but also connect with the divine. Our business is to help people discover the holy within the ordinary relationships of our lives. Our task is to help people relate to the holy, to discover the ultimate in the penultimate. That is, the preacher's job is to help people see God through the four sets of relationships that define human life: history, contemporary world, soul and future (see chapter 4). Every book, every newspaper, every magazine, every phone call, every text message or e-mail message, every encounter with business or family is an encounter with persons in one or more of the four quadrants.

The preacher helps the listener explore the divine that is present in the people who inhabit these four quadrants. Our job is to help people get in touch with the relationships that *are* their lives and to see how God might be present in those to offer strength, healing, encouragement, or abundant life. We are to introduce people in a way that helps others look at them, in them, and through them to the way God is present in their lives. We help people see the holy in the human, the creator in the creation, the mystery in the mundane.

To do this, our first task in a sermon is to develop an introduction. We may begin the introduction one of two ways; with an event or experience that moves toward a thought or idea or with an idea or thought that leads us to wonder about the experience that produced the thoughts. The first appeals to those who relate their way into thinking; the second is of interest to those who think their way into relating. Both honor the integrity between ideas and relationships. Both can function as an introduction of one person to another person.

In many cases our introduction needs to approach the task like we would if we were introducing a stranger to another. To do this assumes that we are dealing with mystery—mystery within each of those who are meeting each other. We do this because our tradition has a strong sense that God is mysterious presence in strangers.

When Abraham and Sarah were getting on in years, they followed the custom of upright people—they welcomed three strangers into their home. As a result of their hospitality, they received the word of divine grace that they would have a child (Gen. 18:1–15). Strangers reveal divine will.

Two disciples, in despair over the death of their Lord, welcomed a stranger on their journey to Emmaus. They invited him to dine with them—fulfilling the responsibility of a good Jew to show hospitality to strangers. In their welcome and in their sharing bread, they discovered the presence of the divine (Lk. 24:13–35). Strangers not only reveal divine will; they also reflect divine presence.

To preach in a way that introduces people to the divine requires that we find ways to introduce people to strangers. But meeting strangers is difficult. It is hard to get started. When I was single I learned that there are many ways to meet strangers, and these have given me clues to how we preachers might introduce strangers to each other in the sermon. A tried and true method of meeting is being "set up" by persons who know both you and the other person. Another old-fashioned way of meeting people was to go out among people and say hello. I was told that I should join groups who were working on something that I enjoyed and to meet people who had something in common with me. Another suggestion was that I get a dog or a baby. I was told that a dog or baby is a great ice-breaker when you're walking in the neighborhood. And I was assured that if I were interested in meeting a woman, a baby or a dog would send the signal that I was a sensitive person—the kind of person a woman might be interested in.

There were more organized ways of meeting strangers. Churches had singles groups whose primary purpose was to create a context in which people could meet. There were also groups that organized speed dating where you go into a room and sit with someone for five minutes and then went onto the next person. The assumption was that within five minutes you could decide if you had enough in common to meet the person again.

There are more high-tech ways to meet people these days. A brief ad in the newspaper personals is rather antiquated. It only gives hints. But Internet dating services will allow you to create a file where your picture and all your vital statistics can be matched with others who have expressed interest in a person like you. Meeting this way does not even require that you go outside the security of your own home.

Now as I reflect on the struggle to meet people, I realize that some of the very same dynamics at work in these ways of meeting are important when it comes to creating an introduction to a sermon. The process of introducing individuals seeking to discover persons with whom they might get better acquainted is very similar to the way we begin a sermon in which we want people to meet persons with whom they might develop a deeper relationship. What are the clues we can gain from personal introductions?

Clarify Expectations

What we expect has a profound impact on what happens in a relationship. When we go to a party, it is important to know if the purpose of going is to meet and mix with important people we are trying to influence for some cause we have or if we are going simply to hang out and enjoy the friendships. If we go to church and expect to be inspired, and all that happens is that we meet friends and listen to ideas about God, that will impact what we get out of it or what we are willing to put into it in the future.

Expectations affect relationships within sermons too. If we are long-term members of a church and listen to sermons, the chances are that we will hear about people we have known and admire. We will hear of Jacob, Ruth, Paul, and Miriam. We will hear of people whose names are familiar, people we know something about. People who attend church regularly often come expecting to hear of the familiar and friendly.

If, however, we hear of a stranger, we may be caught off guard. If we go expecting to hear about Peter's courage and faith—and instead hear of Peter's fear and anger—we might have to adjust our expectations. We can do that. But sometimes we may not have the energy or desire to make that adjustment, and so we may have a hard time listening to the sermon. When preachers help people meet strangers, they need to alert us to the potentially strange.

In my previous book *Living with Loss*,[1] I wrote about anger as a dimension of processing loss. It was not difficult for me to reference Jesus' feeling of abandonment as an illustration of anger. But when the editor read the book, she suggested that I clarify the statement because there would be readers who would quit reading if they saw Jesus' response "My God, My God, why have you forsaken me" as a sign of his anger. If the reader expected Jesus to not experience the emotion of anger and I introduced this strange perception of him without a clarifying expectation, I would lose the reader.

This is true in sermons as well. When we introduce people to strangers, it is important that we clarify the expectations. "Sounds of Silence," (chapter 7) for instance, begins by naming what could be a typical association of Elijah with success and achievement, his struggling with the gods of culture and his own God demonstratively backing him up in the fight. That sermon taps such expected associations in order to pave the way for another stage in Elijah's journey: that of depression and complaining to God. That way-paving signals that a "stranger" or unfamiliar side of Elijah is coming and establishes some guidelines or expectations for what listeners are about to hear.

It is also important to prepare the listener for a sermon as a medium to facilitate healing relationships. If a listener believes that a sermon is where the preacher will answer all the questions of life, she will be very disappointed if she does not get answers. If however she believes that life is not something to find answers for but is about discovering God in the messy, mixed-up relationships that we have, she will listen differently to the sermon. If she believes that she can discover how to live her life of faith fully, she will listen to the preacher, not for answers, but for companionship, and as she makes her discovery. One way to do this is simply state what you do not intend to do in this sermon.

Another way to do this is to begin the sermon by qualifying what you are going to say and do a little reminding of things that are important but are not going to be the focus for today. I preached an ordination sermon in which I wanted to focus on the power of the minister being present to the present. I constructed the following as a part of the sermon's beginning:

I thought I might say to you these words: "Embrace the Future." After all, you are in a major transition in your life. Like Phillip, you are fresh from the womb of Seminary nurture and are heading into the bright light of world struggling to be born as an ordained minister. Something really important is ending. You are leaving behind people who have woven their very souls into your spirits. But, the future is open for you.

And you have to dream. You must have a vision of what is next. It is a vision that seduces and draws you like a magnet to the future. It bends your vision of tomorrow even if you do not know exactly what it will look like. Those who know say that it is really important to cut out pictures and image what you see yourself becoming. Only when you have a clear vision of it can you focus in a way to bring it about.

So, I thought this might be something important to say.

But, then I realized that you already know that. You already know that the future is a powerful lure. You know its terror and the ecstatic energy that it pumps you are your blood stream. You know the ache in your solar plexus when you realize that you do not have a clue what post graduation is going to look like. You know the empty anxiety of a blank future.

So, I decided I would not say this to you.

As my heart beat in the rhythm of my grandson's pulse, I remembered what it was like to sit and hold his mother when she was his age. I remember the contentment and the sense of deep joy I knew raising my three children. I remembered the struggles and the parties of life and gave thanks for them—gave thanks to that amazing reality of existence, which creates, and holds us more tightly than we can ever hold those we love.

And I thought, "Talk today about gratitude. Talk of remembering the friends they have made in seminary and the professors who have given them some insights which they will remember into the future."

This seemed important to say to you because our memory of our lives is what shapes our self-understanding. Events occur. But it is what we remember that give us a sense of who we are. Our memory is a mirror. It reflects to us how others have seen us and therefore how we see ourselves.

And our memory is the treasure chest holding the stones from which our present is being built. It is the foundation–the foundation of both stones and gems. Some of the stones are just gray and boring living–dailyness of existence. Some of the stones shine because they are precious–they hold significance shaped and polished by the heat of passion or pain.

But, I decided that I didn't need to tell you this. After all, this is what every preacher speaks about when she wants you to give money to the church. Gratitude for what we remember is powerful. It is so powerful that it is what we do in many churches weekly to remind ourselves of God's grace–we gather at a table of remembrance.

And we call it sacrament. Memory is sacramental. It is a medium of divine love. It is a means by which we are touched to the very core and weep tears of joy and sorrow as all that we remember has moved on. It is sacramental because memory becomes the reality–it embodies the presence of all those people who have touched our lives in the past.

But I decided not to say this because you already know it.

To begin a sermon by honoring things that might matter and then setting them aside to focus on something else gives the listener a sense of participation in the process. It helps them understand that you are not ignoring some of these valuable issues. You recognize their importance, but you have chosen to focus on something else.

Meeting these strangers may also be dangerous to the listener's status quo. The transforming power of strangers to whom we show hospitality is significant. When we genuinely welcome persons into our lives, we not only open ourselves to giving of ourselves to them, but we open ourselves to receive from them. We open ourselves to take seriously their lives, their histories, and their commitments. When we incorporate new persons into our lives, we can guarantee that we will be changed.

The listener also needs to be alerted to the surprising possibilities that will grow out of this hospitality. When we welcome new people into our lives, we have no idea what the consequence of that relationship might be. In college I took a philosophy class taught by Professor Robert Simpson with no idea what that would do to me. Dr. Simpson introduced me to Kant, Camus, Sartre, and other philosophers who scrambled my way of looking at the world. When I met Dr. Simpson, I had no way of knowing how the relationships he facilitated would change me. I did not know that these thinkers would make it very difficult for me to converse with people who had been my primary community during my childhood and teen years. I did not know that those relationships were forming me into someone unacceptable to some who had nurtured me. Meeting and being transformed by strangers can be dangerous to what we value.

Because of this surprising dimension of welcoming strangers into relationship with us, preaching to facilitate transforming relationships is different from motivational speaking. Motivational speakers will take good ideas, tell you to implement those ideas in your life, and assure you that the consequences will be desirable. The predictable, desirable consequences of your changed behavior serve as motivation for working on change. Preaching for transformation does not guarantee a certain outcome; it simply guarantees that you will be changed.

The preacher has the privilege of inviting the listener into an adventure of discovery. She introduces the listener to new people who will open up a world to them that they cannot imagine. "Sounds of Silence" taps the experience of discouraged, no-words-for-it, cave dwelling by telling the stories of Elijah's cave as well as my own cave encounters with the divine. Neither of these promise a certain kind of reward or resulting relationship with God. These caves can ring sympathetic notes in the listener though, and that sympathy-relationship could help listeners glimpse the blossoms from ashes (closing imagery) and unknown potential that might emerge in their lives as well. It is an exciting discovery to see what can emerge from knowing new people.

Do Not Push

It is important not to be pushy when we introduce people. If we are too anxious for people to meet and like each other, we can distort the process. When we work too hard, pressing each to get acquainted, we can make them uncomfortable and subvert the very process we are trying to facilitate.

In the introduction, the preacher's anxiety can create anxiety in each of the two people we are introducing. If we who are facilitating the introduction are anxious, we are likely to be tense and overplay the introduction. If we are anxious because we want our two friends to like each other, we may overemphasize the dimensions that they have in common. If we are anxious that they hit it off and squeeze us out of the equation, we might end up giving them only a little of what we know so that they will need us to be present for them to continue growing their relationships. So our fear of what we might lose or our fear of what each might lose if they don't hit it off will distort the introduction.

Anxiety in the development of the relationship can choke off our freedom to see and discover the multiple dimensions of the other. When we are anxious, we are not open to the elements that might decrease the anxiety. So if we are anxious around people who do not think as we do, we will be particularly sensitive to differences. For example, if we are anxious Democrats, and we discover that the other person is a Republican, we might not hear the truth about what they are saying. Once they label themselves and the label triggers perceptions about people that we fear or hate, we might close ourselves off to dimensions that we could enjoy and appreciate.

Gary's son Michael just graduated from college. Michael wanted desperately to return to his home city to teach. In an effort to facilitate that on behalf of his son, Gary went to the superintendent of schools and asked him to consider Michael. He called him several times to encourage attention to Michael. But in the process of Gary's campaign on behalf of his son, he pushed too hard. He spoke of Michael in glowing terms. He told him of his intelligence, commitment, childhood, and college credentials. He pushed Michael so hard that the superintendent became suspicious. The opening that was available for Michael went to someone else primarily because Gary pushed too hard.

Most preachers believe that when a person meets and gets to know Jesus there will be healing dimensions to that relationship. Because we believe this, we sometimes try too hard and push people to pay attention or to accept the grace that Jesus offers them. Sometimes we speak in such glowing terms of Jesus that it is almost unbelievable to persons with no relationship with him. Because listeners are aware that Jesus is a stranger, it is important to give them room to welcome the stranger at their own pace. Listeners must get an opportunity to develop their own relationships.

Aside from the danger of pushing people away by our enthusiasm, we should also hold ourselves back because each relationship has its own process, its own dynamic. Each person in a relationship responds according to her comfort level. Some people easily engage new people, while others are slow and need time and space to warm up to people. When we introduce persons to each other, we have to trust that relationship and let it take its own time and course.

We must also respect the fears of the other. One term that is often used in dating relationships is "commitment phobia." This is a term applied to the fear of committing oneself to another. Among some people it is a derogatory term. It is frequently applied to men who do not want to get married, but it is equally applicable to women who may fear getting involved with someone else.

When you understand the power of human relationships, you can understand why persons fear commitment. The relationships we have—the deep and sustaining connections we have over time—will change us. The presence of another person in our lives—a person who expects something from us and from whom we expect something—changes the way we live. If we are not feeling strong enough to face the change, we will stay away.

But we change. Whereas at one point we are not up to paying the price of commitment, at another point we may do it gladly. I know a young woman who became pregnant. She explained how she came to the decision to get pregnant. She became aware in herself of the desire to give up the freedom that she had enjoyed as a woman without children. She decided she would not miss the ability to go out at a moment's notice. She decided that a new life in her home was more important than single freedom.

Most of us do not simply decide to change our lives. We do not simply decide that we want to make a commitment to a relationship—whether to a contemporary relationship or to a relationship grounded in some ancient story. What we realize is that we are willing to give up some of the other relationships and the benefits of those relationships for this one. Overcoming commitment phobia is related to the ability to let go of something that has been important for the sake of something else that you desire more. To do this is to grieve. To do this is to mourn the loss of what you had known. It is to learn how to live without that which was, at one time, very important to you.

When we invite people into healing relationships, we understand that rather than pushing people, we must seduce them. We can tease people into the possibility of the new relationship—to imagine benefiting more from the new relationship than they have from the old relationship. Fear of commitment in the church is well founded. People know that if they commit themselves to a loving relationship with these people, this family—ancient and contemporary—that they will have to give up something that they have cherished—something that has sustained and nurtured them and by which they have known themselves.

When you invite others into relationship with Jesus Christ, you must help them see the invitation to gain with an awareness of the loss. Honest exploration of what they will be giving up is important so that they do not think you have misled them. Being in relationship with a loving, grace-filled reality will change them and result in their becoming a person that they do not yet know. They will become people who love themselves and do not beat themselves up for making mistakes. They will become people who know themselves as acceptable, rather than guilty and burdened with anxiety.

Nonetheless, it is hard giving up the old self. It is hard to live with yourself when you do not feel that tension and burden of guilt. Some think that might be a gift—and it is. But when you have lived with tension in your bones for forty-five years, it is hard to become familiar with yourself as a relaxed person. Fundamentally, you have to learn to love a stranger. The skills that you have developed in loving strangers become helpful in learning to love yourself as a new person.

To introduce people to a stranger with the confidence that the relationship will develop on its own, honors the uniqueness of the listener. When we honor the listener, they will be more open to our suggestions and our insights. When we introduce strangers with the trust that the relationships will develop at their own pace, we are less anxious and more at ease. When we work too hard, our own anxiety can become a barrier to the natural development of the relationship between the listener and the stranger.

When developing an introduction to a sermon, we should not push but invite people to become acquainted with the person we desire them to get to know. If we think it might be helpful for persons in the congregation to know Elijah and his fear when he had been successful against Jezebel, it is important to be careful to let them discover a little at a time (see chapter 7, "Sounds of Silence"). Invite them to imagine what it is like to have faced their fears and then still not been contented or satisfied. Invite them to wonder why they worked so hard to accomplish their goal only to discover that it did not bring them peace.

In introducing people in a sermon, invite but do not push.

Exploring Common Ground

Instead of pushing people to become acquainted, enter the sermon as one who is interested in wondering and musing about things. In the introduction of a sermon, begin with a spirit of exploration. When you introduce friends to each other, encourage exploration of what each party might have in common.

I have a friend who loves horses. When I introduce her to another friend, I will identify a common interest in horses. This kind of introduction helps put persons at ease. If I believe that the person I am meeting has something in common with me, I am more likely to seek to discover more similarities. Discovering similarities creates connection.

I remember when my wife, Deborah, and I had our first lunch date. We told each other about ourselves and were stunned at how many experiences we had in common. We were drawn into each other's life as we shared our journeys. We felt understood because the other had similar experiences.

When we are preaching a sermon and want the listeners to connect with a biblical character, we begin with some common experiences. In "Leaving Home," (chapter 1) I introduced the listener to Moses. I realized that most listeners would have a limited image of Moses. If they knew anything at all, they probably knew of Moses as a leader who liberated the Hebrews from Egyptian slavery. But I wanted them to know Moses as a human who struggled much they way we do. So I began talking of Moses as my friend who was just living life the way each of us do, one day at a time doing what he was paid to do. I wanted the listener to get in touch with the ordinariness of Moses, so they could see him as a potential companion for their journey of faith.

Beware of Title

The way I perceive and articulate people's common interests determines how the introduction goes. If I introduce one of my horse friends as an expert on horses and the other feels they are simply novices at the equestrian enterprise, they may be intimidated. That intimidation will then shape the development of the relationship.

This happens too often when we introduce characters in the Bible. We depict Biblical characters as saints and heroes.

This determination shapes the way the listener relates to the person you are introducing them to.

For example, to introduce the Apostle Paul as "Saint Paul" stacks the deck against equality. If I have never met Paul and know nothing about his life journey–but you tell me he is a saint before you tell me anything else about him–then I am going to immediately determine that this person is not one with whom I can be honest. My perception of what it is to be a saint will affect how I will be able to speak to him and how I will respond to what he says.

If I believe that saints are persons who are "too good to be true" then I will likely withhold information about myself that would reflect my sinful and self-serving self. If I believe that a saint is one who does not get his soul dirty with the complexities of human avarice and intrigue, I will be reluctant to share my own struggles.

On the other hand, if I believe that a saint is one who is superior in service to the poor–as Mother Teresa has often been portrayed–I will discount what she has to say to me because she is different from me. We are not made of the same flesh or tempted by the same demons. Recent revelations of the Mother Teresa's struggle with doubt and confusion in the dark shadows of her own soul will help the listener identify with her. But those stories must be told if the listener is going to be able to be open to a healing relationship with Mother Teresa.

The use of negative titles also distorts the introduction. If I introduce a person as cruel and deceptive, the person to whom I am introducing them might also immediately discount what they have to say. Judas is one who in the history of the church has embodied the fundamental rejection of the holy in human life because of his betrayal of Jesus. When his name is spoken in an introduction, most people already have an image of cruelty and betrayal with which they do not want to associate themselves. His name is synonymous with betrayal. Therefore, it is hard to see our own inclination toward thinking of betrayal when we hear of him.

So when you are introducing people to each other, it is important to let the truth of who they are precede the prejudice that titles might give.

Develop Trust

Understanding of the way our words predispose persons to hear the stories we tell suggests that "trust" is a critical component of the introduction of persons to others who might offer them insights into life. If I am perceived by a listener to be a trustworthy person, she might listen to my story about another person with respect and interest. Trust is grounded in a history. People "trust" persons who have proven trustworthy or who are perceived as part of a trustworthy profession. If the listener has been lied to by a minister in his past, he may not listen very intently or seriously to you as a minister. But if ministers have been truthful previously, people will trust other ministers to tell them the truth as well.

I think that one of the fundamental problems with preaching is that many people do not believe that ministers tell the truth. It is not that they have known ministers to blatantly tell untruths, but some sermons tend to oversimplify life. This builds distrust among persons who know life to be complex.

For example, if a preacher tells a listener that he will become wealthy if he simply gives a thousand dollars to the ministry of the church and the man does not become wealthy, the man will feel the preacher lied. If we tell the listener that prayers will heal persons and they are not healed, listeners will feel that we have deceived them. Exaggerating the truth can create as much distrust as saying something that is blatantly false.

Also if we create an impression that to change your life will bring you the good life and we do not tell the truth about the struggle that will be required, we will not be trusted. I am continually troubled by the ease with which some preachers invite persons to allow Jesus to become Lord of their life. They lead people to believe that this change in their life will bring joy and happiness. But they do not mention the pain and grief that will result when a new convert tries to change the way she lives her life. They do not alert the new Christian to the people who will become frustrated and angry with her if she decides to live her life in support of different values than she did before.

So to introduce persons to one another in a way that might facilitate a saving relationship requires speaking truthfully about both parties. This requires that the person who is preaching and making the introductions know enough about both parties to know where a point of contact might be made. We will explore more deeply the way trust works in relationships in the next chapter.

Common Commitments

Another way to help people connect is by being involved with some of the same commitments. When I watch my grandson, John, in his karate class, I sit with other people who have relatives taking the class. We already have some common points of contact. The karate class might be the reason we are each there, but it is more. We are there because we care about some young person who is learning the discipline of the ancient art of living. We care about him enough to drive and wait for him to finish; or we have deep affection for him and long for him to develop a life of self-control and strength. Because of our commitment to this kind of life, we may have something in common with others sitting in the stands watching the kids go through their routines.

In the sermons in this book, the listeners, the biblical characters and I all share a common desire to experience the divine presence. We all share the desire to seek after, wrestle with or wait for God. In "Leaving Home," (chapter 1) I introduce Moses as one who was committed to life as he had known it, working with the sheep, serving his family and keeping his head down. I desire to help the listener identify with Moses in the ordinary things of life. The listener and Moses and I all share a common commitment to living our lives well. We also can gain insight into our lives as we see what happened to Moses and how he responded to the disruption of his efforts.

Proximity

Introduction of persons to saving relationships also requires proximity. It is hard to be introduced to someone when you do not share the same space. Telling stories about another person is a way of bringing persons into proximity with each other. But to help a person really know the other, you have to share something of the context of the story.

For example, if I told you that my son developed a curriculum for a church camp, you would know that he has some interest in church, young people, and summer conferences. But if I do not tell you other stories about him, you have no idea where he is and what provoked his interest in young people and why he acted to create the curriculum. It is important for me to fill the details if you really are going to be acquainted with my son.

This is also true when you introduce people to each other in a sermon. If you introduce someone like Peter, you will tell a particular story. Most preachers ground their sermons in scripture, and it is usually divided into different stories. You may be preaching about Peter's swim to the beach when he discovered that the man walking on the water was Jesus. An event is the occasion to introduce him, but it is important to then fill in some of the background of who Peter is and tell some of the other stories so that the listener can understand this action in light of Peter's character.

If you do not put Peter's story in the context of Peter's life, then the story can mean anything. You may do a sermon on impulsive behavior and use his actions to illustrate that. But unless you couch the story in the larger understanding of what brought Peter to this point, you distort his true character and the relationship that could develop between Peter and the listener.

The same is true if you introduce the listener to a person who is a contemporary. If you tell the story of a man at the post office sitting outside the door with dark glasses and a white cane and brooms in his lap, you can use him as an illustration of the initiative of "differently-abled" people. But if you want his life to mean something to us, it will require your stopping and getting acquainted with him so you can tell us more about who he really is and what led him to this point of sitting outside that post office.

Humility

Humility is the fundamental attitude of the preacher who wants to introduce people to each other. In the X that is outlined in "How Relationships Heal and Transform" (chapter 4) there are many people and voices in each quadrant. The further from the center of the X we go, the further into mystery we travel. The ultimate mystery out beyond the little that we know and identify is what holds the life that we live. It is what we call God.

Because we approach the people in the Bible and in church history with humility, we introduce them with that same humility. We know some about them, but there is much we do not know. When we introduce them to the persons in the pew, those persons may make discoveries about those characters that we never noticed. When I was in seminary, I was introduced to white men (such as Karl Barth, Rudolf Bultmann, Paul Tillich, and Dietrich Bonhoeffer) from western Europe who helped me see biblical characters through their eyes. But as I have spent a lifetime getting more and more acquainted with those biblical characters, I have discovered the limited relationships that those white western European men had. As I have met persons living in the barrios of South America, I have discovered they have a different perspective on the Bible with different relationships with the characters. As I have come to know women from the African American community, I have discovered how limited my relationship was with the saints compared to theirs.

These and other discoveries have led me to approach my job as a preacher with a great deal of humility. Because I have found biblical characters helpful in my journey toward a fullness of life, I feel compelled to share my relationships with others so that they might make similar discoveries. But I have come to approach it with more humility than I did earlier in my life, saying: "Here's what happened to me and because of what I felt and thought, I made these discoveries. I can't guarantee that you will make these discoveries, but I would like to invite you into my story and explore these relationships with me. Maybe you will make discoveries that will bless your life in ways that will help you live with more courage and faith."

We are transformed by relationships with others. Our relationships with strangers open us up to the strangers within the four quadrants that make up the self. Preaching begins by introducing us to the other with the confidence that the Other will be made manifest in the relationship. We approach the preaching of a sermon with humility and integrity, exploring with the listener the possibilities and discoveries that we have made in our journeys of discovery. We tease them with the possibility that they too might make discoveries that will heal their lives if they take time to deepen their relationships with all the characters within the four quadrants of their life.

Chapter 10 will explore ways that the sermon might facilitate the deepening of the relationships that can heal the listener.

9

The Reluctant Pilgrim Sermon

Sacred Memory

Lk. 1:46–56

The spiritual pilgrimage begins with a burning passion, a passion seeded in the mystery of pain or in the desire of dream. It is a burning that causes us to leave the safe and comfortable mental and emotional structures that have sustained us. It is a burning that calls us to travel, to journey, to discover the Divine and the stranger, to discover God in the cave.

What distinguishes a pilgrim from a tourist is a sense that along the way and at the end, there are hidden strangers who represent the Holy; that there is, even in the silence, divine comfort; that the Holy is in the sacred sight of the memories to which we journey and the dreams to which we drive.

We see many reluctant pilgrims on the road, but there are times on our journeys when we walk alone, for every spiritual pilgrimage in and of itself is a journey of the soul. I have heard suggested that if you find yourself following a path that already exists, it is probably not your path. We spend time walking. Pilgrimages are journeys that are taken slow and steady, sometimes with our shoes off. They are journeys that we take in the midst of the awe and mystery that surrounds us in the life that we have been given.

You walk. The earth rises in its dust to assault your nostrils, and sometimes even boredom trudges beside you. You put one foot in front of the other. You know that you are on a spiritual journey when all you can do is simply take the next step. And as you walk, you walk long enough and alone enough to begin to hear an ache escaping, a groan, a desire. And as you walk, it turns into a sort of beelike hum: first a note or two; then a melody; and then a song begins to rise within you. Reflecting the beat of your feet (sometimes weary and dreary, sometimes staccato and fast as you move) the song begins to rise.

Every pilgrimage is accompanied by a song. Phil Cousineau in *The Art of Pilgrimage*, says that all of the ancient pilgrims who traveled these lands traveled with a song, as they paddled their strokes across lakes, as they walked across mountains."[1] One of our ancient ancestors, Mary, the mother of Jesus, began her reluctant pilgrimage with a song. Some may wonder why I call Mary a reluctant pilgrim, for sometimes Mary is portrayed as one who willingly and happily submitted to the will of the Holy. But the way I have read the Scripture, it appears to me that Mary had some real reservations. You will remember how the angel appeared to Mary and said, "Mary, guess what? You're going to have a baby." Almost all spiritual pilgrimages in the Bible belong to people whose journey began when God disrupted that which they were doing. Mary's life was disrupted. "You're going to have a baby." We are told the first thing she did was ponder these thoughts in her heart. I do not know about you, but when I begin to ponder, it usually is about that which has changed, disrupted the way I was going. It is about something that really matters, something I have to pray about.

Mary worried about these things, and she felt inadequate. She says, "What do you mean, I'm going to have a baby? I can't have a baby. I am a virgin." Not unlike Moses who said, "Who am I that I should go?" The saints, when disrupted and called by God to do something out of the ordinary, have always been reluctant to respond and have sought any excuse that they could to ignore the call.

However, Mary did more than worry and find excuses. Mary went to see her kin, Elizabeth, a woman not unlike Mary, who had her life disrupted. She was not a young woman and a virgin, but an old woman and barren. Her life changed when she was told by the same God, "You're going to have a baby." Mary took her pondering, her worrying to the wisdom of the aged.

When we find ourselves called on a pilgrimage, one of the first places to go is to consult with the wise, those who have been there, those who know what it is to have a dream and have a dream die. To begin a pilgrimage is to consult with those who know. I found on my pilgrimage that there were counselors who traveled with me. Pastors and friends did not let me sit alone all the time in my cave, but walked with me and were still and let me listen.

I also found counselors and guides who came to me in books. Gerald Sittser, in *A Grace Disguised*,[2] tells the story of the loss of part of his family and how he struggled to make sense of their tragic deaths at the hand of a drunk driver. I discovered in Mr. Sittser a companion on my journey. And Belden Lane, in *The Solace of Fierce Landscapes*,[3] explores mountain and desert spirituality as he sits with his mother who is dying of cancer. These are friends to whom I went and found comfort and guidance as I made my way on the pilgrimage toward new life.

After Mary went to Elizabeth, we are told that she began to sing. Mary sang a song. It was not a narrative; it was a song. Mary began to sing a song that she knew from her sister who lived hundreds of years earlier, Hannah. Hannah had discovered what it was to give birth to one who would help the oppressed, one who would hear the pain and the cry, and respond to God. Mary sang her sister's song.

Songs are often brief history lessons. Songs frequently embody the stories that define who we are. I know many people in congregations I have served whose theology was not shaped by reading Karl Barth or by reflecting on some theologian; their theology was shaped by the hymns of the church. Songs shape the soul because they are stories that are embodied and implanted deep within the psyche. Stories, when they are sung, nourish our spirits and warm our hearts.

Recently my wife, Deborah, and I went down to southern Indiana to Brown County and spent a couple of nights in a cabin. In southern Indiana we have what we call mountains. They are actually just hills, but we even have a ski resort (with homemade snow) in southern Indiana. In the cabin, a great glass wall looked down on the naked, empty trees of winter.

I built a fire in a potbellied stove in the middle of the room. We sat in front of the fire, wrapped a quilt around our shoulders, and felt the heat on our faces. It was cold behind us in the dark, but our faces were warm from the fire. I remembered our ancient mothers and fathers who used to gather around campfires and tell stories, warmed by the stories of the fire and cold on their backs as they are enveloped by the black night beyond the campfire circle. I watched the fire burn.

But in the silence of those Indiana hills, we also heard the fire sing. It popped and cracked, and it sang its notes and pitches. I began to think, "Yes, the fire is singing its story, for what are these logs but stories packed in circles, chopped up in short log." This tree has seen decades of life go by its trunk and under its outstretched branches. Decades of pilgrims have walked beside it. It has stories to tell, and it is broken and cut and piled up with other logs. In the heat of the fire, it sings its song. We sat and were warmed by the stories of the pilgrims who had walked the hills of southern Indiana.

We sing our stories. They warm our hearts. But we sing also for memory. We sing also to remember that we are one with someone who is other than us, but who is us—with strangers whom we do not know, but whom we do know. Mary sang a song of identification—of identification with all of her sisters who were oppressed, with all of her brothers who were put down, with all of the slaves of her history. She identified through song, a song that wrapped itself around her and warmed her like a quilt, a quilt of memory.

The songs we sing are ways in which we identify ourselves and gain strength from those who have gone before. Songs help us sort out the threads of our lives and pull them up so we can weave them into some new life. Songs help us find the notes that are dancing around deep within our spirits in chaos and help put them in order so that they make meaning of our lives.

Not long after my first wife died, my son was going back to college, He needed a car–he needed *my* car. I told him that he could have it. In an effort to facilitate that transfer of my transportation, he went with me to buy a new car. After we picked out the car I wanted, we sat down in the showroom. The salesman asked, "Do you want a moon roof on your car?" I said, "I don't know," and Stephen said, "Yes, he wants a moon roof." The salesman then asked, "Do you want a CD player?" I said, "No, I don't have any CDs." Stephen said, "Yes, he wants a CD player, because he'll have CDs."

My son was leading me in directions I did not want to go, but in the end, Stephen was right. The car became my sanctuary, and CDs helped me learn my new song. My kids sent me CDs to help me along the way. They sent me songs they thought would help me travel on my journey. They sent me songs of love that made me weep. They sent me songs with harsh, loud, and angry words that made me scream. I remember driving through the back roads, with my moon roof open, with Delbert McClinton singing hard, southern rock, raw and rash. And I stuck my fist through the roof, and my anger and my frustration spilled out into the sky. The songs brought from me that anger that was stirring and depressing my soul and named it, so that I could weave it into the world that was coming, so that I could create a new world symphony for me to sing. We sing in order to find the notes within us so that we can write our new song.

Several years ago I traveled with a group from our seminary to Ghana. There were thirteen of us on this trip, eleven African Americans and two Anglo Americans. We were traveling together on a hot bus. How hot? I do not know. I kept asking how hot, and they said, "It's hot." "But how hot?" "Well, it's just hot." And it was. As we traveled together our patience wore as thin, as the tires bounced over dirt roads. Being on the bus was interesting because I was in the minority–a way of living that is rare for me. I was one of only three Anglo Americans.

Many of my African American colleagues were singing songs. Their stories were punctuated with songs and scriptures. It was a colorful experience. Occasionally I tried to tell my story, but I just could not get it in. I did not know how to get it in. I felt left out. I know they did not intend to leave me out. It was simply the culture. It was the way they did things, and I was so colorless. It was an incredible experience, one that has transformed my understanding of what it means to be excluded, not intentionally but simply by the nature of the way life is structured.

One of the places we traveled was to a slave castle on the coast—a castle where hundreds of thousands of human beings were stashed in rooms waiting to be transported all over the world. I went to this place of torture with my African American brothers and sisters. We walked where my colleagues' ancestors had walked. We went into dungeons where men and women had been stacked so tightly that they could not lie down. When people died they simply stood on top of the dead. The dead rotted into the soil.

We walked on that ground, and we were stunned as we walked through "the door of no return." I saw pride begin to rise in my African American brothers and sisters as they returned through "the door of no return." Something happened while we were walking on those sacred and hollow grounds. We no longer were tourists, but we became pilgrims. After we had toured the dungeons together, we came out into the sunlight. We stood silent, wondering what to say. No words were adequate. Then one young woman began to sing this song:

> Lift every voice and sing til earth and heaven ring.
> Ring with harmonious liberty.
> Let our rejoicing rise high as the listening skies.
> Let it resound loud as the rolling sea.
> Sing a song full of faith that the dark past has taught us.
> Sing a song full of hope that the present has brought us.
> Facing the rising sun of our new day begun.
> Let us march on til victory is won.[4]

And as she began to sing, other voices chimed in. And I was a part of one body of memory, and power, and identification. I was, as an Anglo American, walking in a pilgrimage of pain with my brothers and sisters of African descent. The music spoke the memory, and it bound us together in a common identity with those who had gone before. It planted its power in our souls, for we were not singing simply about the past, but we were singing about the future. At the end of the song, we shouted together, "Never again! Never again!"

10

Deepening Relationships in the Body of the Sermon

Preaching has a bad name in many circles. I heard a discussion in a wedding that I attended. A person was celebrating that the preacher *did not* preach a sermon. The fact is the preacher *did* preach a sermon. But it was done in a way that resulted in the listener feeling that she had heard a conversation rather than a sermon. For her, a sermon had connotations of heavy-handed "shoulds" and "oughts." Preaching done well is more about discovering and remembering who we are than about telling people who they ought to be. The body of a sermon is designed to deepen the relationship of the listener to the community of faith, creating a sense of identity and self-understanding. By calling those people into presence among the listeners, the spirit and character of the community gives shape and form to the self-understanding of the listeners.

As we have observed, most of us have lists of changes that we "should" make and do not. For the preacher to add to that list and to add his moral weight to the pressure the listener already feels seldom results in transformation. It may result in the listener "trying harder" and even make a temporary change in behavior. But most of us are unable to stick with new behaviors unless we are in relationships that continually reinforce our desire for change. Sermons that develop a deepening of the relationship of the listener, the preacher, and the characters from antiquity or the contemporary world will enhance the possibility for transformation.

A deepening relationship is one where we begin to discover more of what we have in common, but more importantly, how we are different. Where and what we have in common tend to reinforce who we have been; what we discover that is different has the potential to help us grow and change.

When we explore our differences, we get into the things that may be difficult. When we are honest, there will always be points of disagreement with persons we know at a deep level. Conflicts arise because the differences may be in our core values. But the capacity to develop intimacy with another person and know the impact of a deep relationship is related to the ability to know and live with the differences between you.

The differences between us contribute to the healing possibility in relationships. The abundant life is one in which there is great diversity of experience and relationship. Diversity is a strength, not a weakness. A stand of trees that are all the same species is susceptible to disease and destruction. A forest that survives for centuries has a mixture of multiple varieties of trees and plant life. The wildlife that inhabits that forest is sustained by different kinds of life cohabitating the space. When the weather is bad for one kind of plant, another sustains the ecosystem while the one kind of plant is being weak and unproductive.

Human diversity in community is also a strength. A church filled with only young people is no stronger than a church of only older people. Without the diversity of experience and wisdom associated with age, a church becomes susceptible to life-threatening diseases. Churches that are rich with diverse ages, genders, economic conditions, cultural complexities, and histories will have the resources to adjust to changing times.

Deepening a relationship through preaching also requires diversity. For people to be transformed, they must be in relationship with the diverse people who make up the four quadrants of their world. And people do want to change.

It is sometimes assumed that people do not want to change. Sometimes preachers speak as if they are scolding people for not wanting to repent or change to become better persons. I believe that persons who attend church believe that change is one of the reasons they attend. Most people are not so naive as to believe that they will not change. But most people assume change is evolutionary and not revolutionary. We are more likely to accept change that sneaks up on us than change forced upon us.

When I went back to my hometown, it had radically changed. Houses had been torn down and rebuilt. My high school had been demolished, and a new one stood a mile away. The Dairy Queen where I worked had been expanded to include inside seating. Change is so radical. But for those who had lived there for forty years without leaving, the change had been gradual, evolutionary, and almost imperceptible. Most change that people know is subtle; when it is slow and evolutionary, it can usually be embraced.

What are some of the things that sermons must do to develop and deepen relationships so that the change will more likely be embraced?

Evoking Presence

A sermon must evoke the presence of the other. To relate to another creature, they must be present. If relationships offer healing, we must be able to sense the presence of those to whom we are relating. This means we must sense their spirit and their bodies. This does not mean that we must simply relate to those who are physically alive. Mary Helen told me about feeling the presence of her husband long after he died. She could smell his pipe and sense his smile even though he had died two years earlier.

It is possible to be in a room with another and not sense her presence. Many long-term relationships descend to the experience of a "ghost in the chair." The person is there, but he has evaporated into mist. Presence is a power that is known whether or not the person is physically alive.

To preach in a way that facilitates healing relationships, one must develop the ability to evoke the presence of not only those who are in the pew beside the listener, but also to evoke the presence of the saints who live in memory, the spirits that live in the soul, and the community of the future which lives in the imagination (see chapter 4, "How Relationships Heal and Transform"). When I develop a sermon, I seek to evoke presence by reference to concrete, tactile, sensual, and embodied language. These come when I am present to my body. I get some of my best ideas when I am biking, walking, or taking a shower. When I am out of my head and in my body, my mind is free to be visited by new ideas and new associations. When I am obsessed about some idea, my anxiety shuts down the consideration of options. When I relax and try not to force the presence, the idea comes to me. So when I am facilitating the evocative spirit of another, I have to create a sense of relaxed embodiment so that the body might recall and meet the person I am inviting into the conversation.

When we see preaching as evoking the presence of voices already in the listener, we understand our role as helping them gain strength and insight from dimensions of themselves that already inhabit their psyche. We are inviting them to become more of who they are, rather than trying to make them into someone different. It is much easier to become more of who we are than it is to become something entirely different.

In the sermon "Sacred Memory," (chapter 9) I speak of Mary's response to the divine via identification with her sisters by illustrating life stories of southern Indiana folk and the songs of Delbert McClinton. I present these life stories and the raw songs we might already blast from our car stereos–the everyday things of our lives–as if they were sources of wisdom that we brought with us and could listen to or sing with as we become more ourselves by living more fully into what we carry. I do not seek to give us things from outside, foreign things, as if we ought to change or draw on a whole new set of life things. Rather, getting to know this Mary who lives more deeply into the songs of her world helps listeners imagine living more deeply into the songs of our world.

Respect Privacy

One of the ideas that I have to develop in the introduction of a sermon is the dimension of respect for the sacred privacy of another. When I am introducing strangers, I tend to focus on that which I know each might have in common with the other. But I also focus on that which I believe the other would want said. I do not reveal much of what I know—especially that which I think the friend might not want known immediately. For example, I would not introduce one friend to another with the phrase "He can be stingy." I will say things I think the one would want shared.

To give too much information is to deny the persons the right to discover what they can about each other. If I mediate each to the other by telling all I know and finishing all the sentences for each, I deprive them of the freedom to discover what the uniqueness of their relationship might reveal. To give more than a cursory introduction is to presume that you know what each could find out if they had the time to be together.

Individuals in relationship are unique, and each draws something different from the other. I want to introduce people to each other and then let them discover their unique dimensions. That way I also can discover new things about them.

This happens when I get together at holiday with my adult children. As I sit and listen to them talk with each other, remembering experiences and reporting what is happening in their lives, I discover things that I would never know if it were up to me and my unique relationship with each to discover. The joy of preaching in community is that it reveals far more than the limited perspective of a one-on-one relationship could uncover.

So to evoke presence in community is to create a rich and growing space of turmoil and pleasure (see "Postlude"). By creating this encounter of memory and chaos, we contribute to the listener's capacity to develop skills in self-understanding and personal growth. We help her develop her own strength in relationship to the resources she already has available. If the listener comes and expects to hear the answers of the minister rather than to discover the relationships within his own life, he will develop a dependent relationship that will not serve him well in the long run. Helping people discover their inner resources creates stronger, more self-reliant people.

One of the ways we deprive people of the pleasure of their own strength is by appealing to the biblical Eden in memory and the eschatological future of Revelation. This appeal may be important as we imagine the reign of God where the longings of the human heart are satisfied. But if we do not deal with the real possibilities closer to the center of the X, we leave people without the satisfaction of present fulfillment. We must respect the unique sense of authority and power persons have within their own consciousness. When we respect the way people are seeking to fulfill their life of faith, they will be open to suggestions about ways they might expand that life.

In respecting people, we respect their fears. One morning I went to pick up my two-year-old grandson. I live 1,500 miles from him and see him only once every two or three months. I had arrived after he had gone to bed, so he did not know I was there. When I went in to get him out of his bed, I opened the door. In his little long-john grey pajamas, he was on his hands and knees. He looked at me as I said, "Good morning." He looked suspiciously at me, not moving. I moved a little closer and said again, "Good morning." He glanced over at the door to see if anyone else was coming in. After a long moment, he said, "Mommy?" I said, "She's in the kitchen." Another long pause. Then he smiled, stood up and reached out his arms for me to take him.

When we are approaching persons in the space of their soul, it is something like approaching Andrew as he is waking up. For me to have quickly gone in, flipping on the light and loudly announcing that I had come to get him, would have overwhelmed him and not allowed him to ease out of sleep into the safety of his own day.

Sometimes our preaching does not regard the space of others. We do not respect the chaos or the pain they bring to the sanctuary and assume that they are ready to meet the strangers who have come into their spaces. To respect the listeners is to listen to where they are and to introduce other people (and through the presence of other people, introduce them to the Other) in a warm and gentle way. The "Postlude" of this book will explore ways of creating space for these encounters.

Listening

Listening enhances and deepens relationships. The ability to see into a person is related to the ability to set aside our own drives and impulses, getting inside the skin of the other. My daddy taught me, "Don't judge another person till you walk a mile in their shoes."

And it takes time to walk a mile. It takes time to listen to people. We listen over time—in different contexts. To know David, one listens to him as he sings, as he governs, as he plots his intimate relationships, and as he calculates his conflicts. The whole person is complex and diverse and one cannot know David unless he knows him in all of his dimensions.

A therapist will listen over time—listen to recurring themes and concerns and reflect back what she hears—to help the whole person know himself better, not just one layer of a person; it is knowing multiple layers revealed over time in different contexts. This is why it is important for people to hear the same biblical stories over and over. Learning the faith is not something for children to do and then walk away from as adults. The transforming power of the stories of faith comes as the result of hearing them in the different contexts of our lives. To hear the story of the prodigal when we are six is different from hearing it when we are nineteen. At six we may have only dreamed of running away from home. But at nineteen we may have left home and squandered all that we had inherited. To hear it at that point is to know ourselves differently. And then to hear the story again when we are thirty-four and faithful in our commitments to family and work we realize how the older son is more reflective of who we are than is the prodigal son. We discover something new about ourselves. And to listen to the story when our son has rejected all our values and is wandering the globe "seeking himself" is to realize that we are a lot like the waiting father. To know the characters in the Bible and ourselves at a deeper level requires listening over time.

To develop a relationship also requires talking. So a preacher has to create a way in which the listener can talk back. Dialogue in a sermon helps a listener learn how to talk back. When Jesus is in the garden and submitting to the authorities, it is so easy to make that into a scene where Jesus is a lamb being led to the slaughter. But the listener must be wondering—where is the lion that challenged the authorities? Where is the strong person who challenged the moneychangers in the temple? When preaching these texts, it is critical to allow the questions of the listener to inform what one does in the sermon.

One of the ways to evoke this is to allow the characters in the Bible to wonder in their minds. There is no way that we can know fully the emotional and spiritual struggles that biblical characters faced. But we can use our imagination and have the characters come up with questions and thoughts. When the Apostle Paul is involved in the stoning of Stephen, we can have him struggling with himself. We can imagine that he has been shaped by his heritage that is opposed to killing. But we can also have him think of how the purity of the faith must be protected. Internal conversation can take place so that the listener can identify with his struggle—and discover a companion in their own struggle between values that they hold dear.

One of the most important things the preacher must do is to help a listener draw upon the resources that are within him or her. This is facilitated when the preacher realizes that the major conflicts in life are not between good and evil, but between good and good. When we tell the story of Paul and allow him to struggle between the value of life and the value of a sacred community, we allow the listener to identify with the complex nature of decisions and actions. When we reveal this part of Paul's life, we offer the listener a companion in his struggle between two goods.

The preacher must listen to both the person to whom they are preaching and to the characters they are introducing to their listeners. When they listen to the deep struggles and hopes within each, they are better able to facilitate their meeting and deepening of the relationship. When we listen carefully, we can better help them converse with each other.

Wasting Time

To deepen our relationship with the other, we must have time simply designed for the pleasure of being together. When I meditate, I gather myself together in the presence of silence. I learned that meditation does not work, and it is not designed to work. It is not designed to bring you anything except into relationship with presence. When we meditate to get something, we fail. If we meditate to feel better, peaceful, or some preconceived experience of what we hope God will be like, we will most likely be disappointed. The act of meditating becomes work to achieve preconceived goals.

Meditation is being in the presence of God, who is mystery and who is unknown. It is characterized by simply restful waiting—without a preconceived notion of what it might be like to get something. It is about wasting time—wasting time with the secret silence that surrounds us—the silence from which we seek to hide because it scares us. We settle into the silence, not trying to organize it with words or to understand it with language.

In some way, this is one of the characteristics of a healing relationship. It is a relationship that is not designed to do something—it is being in relationship to the other as they are—not for what they can do for us or what we can do for them or even for what we can both do for someone else.

It seems to me that most of our relationships are centered on roles. We have roles to perform, and we hang out with people with whom we can perform those roles. And we get along as long as we can each function in those roles. When I was a pastor, I related to people as a pastor. My relationship with most of those people simply evaporated when I left the parish. We believed that we would remain friends, but that was not the case as much as we expected. Without the common purpose of being in the same congregation, we were not drawn to each other.

My relationship with my children is an example of how our roles define our relationships. When my children grew up, they left home—but I tended to treat them as my children when I saw them. After their mother died, we had to relearn our relationships. I had related to them as part of a partnered team of parents, and they did not know me as a single parent. I did not know myself as a single parent. But as they were away from home and on their own, we had to learn how to relate as humans. We are bound by a common history and bonded by a lifetime of living in certain roles, but now we need to be adult humans independent from each other in ways that we had not been before.

Healing relationships are ones where we are present because of some role we play—husband, wife, parent—but that role can function as a window to see more. There is a better chance for the healing to occur when we have time with each other, particularly time that is not structured.

This seems to be one of the main reasons for the lack of satisfaction in relationships. We do not "waste" time anymore. Everything has to be structured. Children have organized sports, dance, and music. Parents are so structured that they do not have time to simply waste time hanging with their children. The songs that we learn to sing in our organized lives are ones that connect us to others—function to make us better singers—rather than the hearing of the unique soul's song of the individual self.

When we waste time with another, we are exposed to the rich mystery that characterizes who they really are. When we are exposed to their mystery, we are in touch with the ultimate mystery, God, who holds all life. Relationships become stale and uninteresting when they become predictable. They lose mystery when we fail to realize that the other is like an iceberg and that what we see above the water is only a minuscule part of who that person really is.

Time and Patience

If we are free to spend time simply exploring our relationships with others, we are less inclined to rush to judgment. Too many sermons prejudge the idea or the person they are introducing people to. Deductive preaching encourages this. In deductive preaching, a person declares the point to be made and attempts to prove that point. The judgment has already been made.

If we see relationships as the healing factor, we do not know what the point will be until we have had the encounter with the person. And the point will be only what we know because of what happened in that particular encounter at that particular time. Effective preaching will take time and will require patience. If I as a listener am to discover for myself the impact of a certain character within the sermon, I must have the privilege of spending time with that person. If the preacher presumes to already know what that person will mean to me, she has taken away my right to make that discovery for myself.

And if the preacher presumes to know what my relationship with a biblical character will mean to me, there is no room for the life-giving experience of living the relationship. This is the problem with so many "how to" books that I have read on multiple subjects. Some books on marriage seem to know what a couple ought to mean to each other. They prejudge what is good and right on the basis of some preconceived notion of good. But if each person is unique and each relationship is unlike any other, then the only way we will know the meaning of it is to live it and articulate it ourselves. This is why inductive preaching has a greater potential for facilitating and deepening relationships. If we begin with the particular (event, person, issue) and explore the implications with an eye toward what we might discover, we can suspend judgment and allow people to see what makes sense to them in their particular context.

If we spend time in a relationship, not prejudging what it might mean, there is then room for discovery—for more—for the mystery to continue to be revealed. "Sacred Memory" is an entire sermon journey of people spending (or wasting, more to the point) time sharing songs. In that song space Mary ponders, I journey the back roads of existence and a community reclaims from a brutal past their lives together as sisters and brothers. But who knew what the sermon was about until each of those stories were told and songs heard? If we are able to meet and get to know another and suspend judgment, we will be open to the discovery of the mystery that is yet to be revealed. If we judge the relationship before we experience it, we will limit what can be discovered.

Conflict

When we deepen relationships with persons, conflict is an inevitable consequence. Two people who develop a deep degree of intimacy are going to discover that there are significant points of difference.

When my wife and I married (both for the second time), we moved in together after a significant number of years of being single. We love each other deeply and want to share our lives and our space. We want to explore the world together. We love adventure and travel.

But after the first few months of being in the same house, we passed the "honeymoon" period where we each had enough energy to work hard at avoiding those things that might create conflict. But as anyone who has swallowed hard and avoided trouble knows, conflicts eventually reveal themselves. A rich and satisfying marriage includes the capacity to manage conflict.

Conflict is a natural part of life. It is not something that can be avoided (like many in church would do) or resolved (like many in marriages would hope), but it is something being constantly processed. To be alive is to constantly be in conflict. We struggle between life and death, individual and community, loving our children and loving meaningful work. To be alive requires that we constantly choose between one thing and another. We therefore must develop a lifestyle that attends well to the differences reflected in the choices.

Unfortunately, conflict is considered by some to be a danger and a threat. Within many congregations, people fear conflict for they have seen what it can do when it descends into attack and counterattack. As a result, many congregations have avoided intimacy because they have not been able to go through the process of conflict that results from knowing the truth about each other.

But conflict is not only something that is the result of deepening of a relationship; it is the experience of life itself. We are in continual conflict with our past. The future moves in on us and we are constantly negotiating between what worked for us in the past and what will work for us now. There is continual tension created simply by the process of living.

That is why we are so fascinated by novels, theater, movies, and stories. Conflict is required to keep our interest. There must be some tension between what is happening, what has happened, and what might happen. Even the most benign documentary has conflict in it. *The Story of the Weeping Camel* is a beautiful documentary about a camel in the Mongolian desert that gave birth to an albino calf.[1] The story is about the rejection of the calf by her mother, and the struggle of the herdspersons to coax the camel to accept her baby and to nurse her. The conflict between the camel and her calf, between the people and the camel, and the conflict within the moviegoers' hearts as we felt the ache of pain of all the participants, kept us riveted to the movie, anticipating what would happen.

So if conflict is basic to the nature of life and the result of a deepening relationship, preaching that facilitates healing relationships must deal with conflict. Sermons that hope to have an impact on listeners need to have tension and conflict inherent within them or they will be ignored or rejected as Pollyannaish.

And conflict needs to be authentic. It need not be a cartoon conflict. If the only conflict in sermons is between Satan and God, the listeners will soon find the sermons are disconnected from them. For most people do not experience life as radical good and radical evil. Most of us experience life as a mixture of choices—some may be good, some may not be so good, sometimes none of them very good. Sermons that do not introduce listener to characters who are real in all of their complexity will leave the listener wondering where to go for companionship in the journey of faithful living.

This means that our illustrations cannot be constantly comparing and contrasting a Mother Teresa and an Al Capone. Most people do not feel they are capable of being a superstar of goodness or evil, and they will soon tire of feeling that the faith is something unrelated to them.

The conflict within a sermon needs to embody real people who have real problems. This can be done by fleshing out the characters of the Bible so that people can identify with them. One of the reasons Peter is such a popular character in the Christian community is because of his mixture of impulsive rejections of Jesus and his faithful acceptance of Jesus and his way. The reason David is such a beloved character in the Bible is precisely because he is a powerful mixture of good and evil. When I listen to stories about David, I feel the adventure of his life and it hooks the memory of my own collection of good and evil.

Suffering and Struggle

When we get to know the characters of the Bible we discover that one of their common characteristics is that they all struggled: Jacob, Sarah, Abraham, Moses, Saul, Ruth, Tamar,

David, Isaiah, Paul, Martha, Mary, and even Jesus. Temptation and the struggle with the self is a characteristic of the saints in the church. If we are to preach to facilitate healing human relationships, we must share truthful and complex stories about characters who are a part of faith's family album.

Struggling itself may very well mean that the holy is near. When Jacob wrestled with the stranger on his way to see his brother, we discover that it was a holy encounter. When we break bread and drink wine and remember Jesus, we remember the suffering related to the giving of ourselves. We have to break ourselves into roles for different parts of the day and into the diversity of our gifts, and make them as an offering to another. Suffering in relationships often opens us to deeper levels of connection with each other.

Forgiveness

Forgiveness permits one to be present to the present. When we do not forgive, neither we nor those who have offended us are able to be fully present in the moment. When an offense has the power to remain present, it stains the present. The pain of the offense often handcuffs our hearts to the past–making it closed to what is happening now. To grieve is to learn to live in the absence of something significant. To become a new creature, the power of the past must be engaged and expressed and forgiven so we can discover the gifts of today and imagine the gifts of tomorrow.

Therefore, grieving is essential to the self as a growing self. One cannot grow unless one is able to be present to the present, where life is lived. So we cannot be alive nor can we deepen our experience of life if the past is so present that it overwhelms us. To see the present as it is requires the capacity to allow the past to lose its power in controlling how we see the present. That is forgiveness.

If preaching is facilitating healing relationships, it must facilitate growing relationships. It must enable people to forgive those relationships that block the capacity to be present to the now.

And forgiveness happens. It is not something that one so much does as it is something that one recognizes as a gift.

Forgiveness is the capacity to recognize that the past is not as powerful as it used to be. And that is usually related to a sense of security. The ability to let go of that which we know to be our experience of reality is related to our ability to move with courage into the future.

Courage comes when one survives danger. That is why it is so important for persons to be in risky and dangerous situations—discovering the capacity in one's self to live and thrive even when threat is near.

The ability to forgive is related to one's ability to end relationships. It is linked to our ability to end one way of relating to life and begin another way of relating to life. If we believe that life is something that we possess and that our sense of well-being is related to how much we possess—we will have a hard time ending relationships. We will not want to let go of that which we know.

Our ability to end relationships is also related to our confidence in the future to give us new relationships. It also is related to our ability to live within ourselves—to relate to the multiple selves within and discover in the memories and in the soul the presence of those who have gone before. And our ability to end is related to our ability to forgive. If we can forgive the actions of a person in the past, we can end the relationship to the offending events that blind us to the present.

In "Sacred Memory," (chapter 9) Mary sings Hannah's song in the context of the disruption and worry. Hannah had pondered her own experience, where there was a life to forgive for not being as she would thought it would be, a God to forgive for not offering a life she might have expected, and a world to forgive or make some sort of peace with even in the context of the oppression, pain, and tears. Mary's song is the song of women who face major conflict scenarios and manage to sing them, not as threat, but as laden with blessing potential.

Silence

Another characteristic of a deepening relationship is silence. People who are secure in their love for each other and who live in a deepening understanding can often sit in silence and be present. It is not necessary to talk all the time. Too many words deny the people time to soak in each other's presence. Sermons, too, may grow out of the garden of silence. In my sermon "Sounds of Silence," (chapter 7) I sought to create that sense of Elijah's experience of silence in the cave. Words like these, which grow deep roots in the soil of silence are often rich with fruit when they are spoken.

Songs

Music often grows out of deepening relationships. The Bible has sections of songs–songs that express the deep longing of the heart–songs that are honest reflections of centuries of a relationship with God. These songs reflect dimensions of a relationship that is complex and diverse.

Some might suggest that Christians should not sing some of the songs in the songbook of the Hebrew people. Songs that call down pain and suffering on one's enemies are not songs that should be sung by Christians who are charged to love their enemies. At a cognitive level, I understand this objection to some of the Psalms.

But at an emotional level, where deep cries out to deep, I can imagine times when those Psalms express the agony of the singer as thoroughly as a song by Delbert McClinton helps me express my own anger and frustration. In helping the singer identify a passion for hatred and destruction, those Psalms explore ways to respond that could create reconciliation rather than revenge. To deny the passion for revenge assures that it will be woven more deeply in the daily fabric of relationships with all whom we know.

Songs are not doctrinal statements. They are musings of the spirit as it responds to the experiences of our lives. They are therefore as diverse as the human experience. That diversity is a characteristic of the abundant life for which we have been created.

Storytelling

One of the most powerful ways for relationships to deepen is to tell stories. The way humans interact is by telling stories. When I meet a friend for coffee, I ask, "What's happening?" The response is usually a story of something that the person has just been doing or pondering. For example, my friend might say, "My daughter is driving me crazy. She has just announced that she wants to go to the Junior/Senior prom at school. She is only a freshman, and I don't know what to do." The story will continue about how fourteen is just too young to go to a prom with a senior.

My friend will then say something like, "I remember when I was that age. I was asked to a prom, and my dad put his foot down. I hated him for it because he didn't trust me to go out with a boy three years older. I never forgave him for that."

I say, "I went to the Junior/Senior prom when I was freshman class president."

And she says, "But that was different. You are a boy."

I say, "Are there double standards? Do boys take care of themselves better than girls?"

She responds, "I have a friend whose daughter went out with a senior, and they went to a friend's house afterwards. His parents weren't home and they got into the liquor cabinet."

And so it goes; one story after another—each evoking memories of yet another story. Each story hooks memories of people in the four quadrants of our hearts. When preachers tell stories, they help deepen the relationship the listener has with the characters in the scripture.

But each story is not simply drawing from the contemporary quadrant and the historical quadrant. The story also draws from the soul quadrant. The deep love the mother has for her daughter is hooked and comes out dressed in the clothes of fear that her daughter might get in trouble or be involved with people who will take advantage of her. As I listen to my friend tell her stories, I get to know her soul—her heart's desires and fears, her aches and her agony.

I also get to know the longings of the future quadrant that whisper her into tomorrow. I glimpse her hopes for her daughter that she can make it into adulthood without being hurt too badly. I sense that she has an image of what might be best for her daughter as she faces her future. I become aware of my friend's imagination as it spins out one scenario after another.

This same deepening occurs when we tell stories of the biblical characters. In *Story Journey: An Invitation to the Gospel as Storytelling,* Thomas E. Boomershine tells the story of the birth of Jesus. He outlines the story in Luke as it begins with the experience of enrollment, moves toward the journey to Bethlehem, introduces the shepherds and their encounter with the angels, confirms the angels' story by having the shepherds visit the manger, and then provides a moment of reflection on the responses of amazement and quietude.[2]

Boomershine tells the story and its context of oppression, shame, and inhospitality. He evokes not only a sense of the story as it is told in the Bible, but also the stories of the listener's shame, rejection, and oppressive burdens are invoked. As one is told of a young mother finding a way to take care of her child in a place that had no room for her, it evokes stories within the listener's own world where people have had courage to give birth, swaddle, and care for rejected ideas and dreams. When we tell the stories of the community, we evoke memories and emotions that have shaped us in our past and whose presence within us will shape how we live in the future. The people evoked in the stories that are told and heard will transform us.

Each relationship we have has the possibility of growing deeper. The preacher can facilitate that deepening by invoking the presence of others through respect, listening, grace-filled storytelling. When we have a deeper and more significant relationship with people, there is a greater potential for transformation.

11

Coming Home

Mk. 14:22-25

It has been a journey this week, a journey from deep burning, the burning of one who was unsatisfied sitting on the hillside tending sheep. It has been a journey through stranger to friend and friend to stranger, a journey where we have glimpsed the smile of God in the cave of silence, and have heard the voices of the Divine in the ancient mentors and in our memory of music.

But now it is time to go home. It is time to move on. It is time to lean toward that which accepts and embraces us for who we are. It is time to move ahead and to find a place to sit for a while. But it is not always easy to leave the road. Some of us are going to have a hard time leaving here to go home.

I have been wandering for seven years in my journey of faith. I have had the good fortune of having ancient pilgrims teach me. I have had an occasional glimpse of God, but never God's face, only the backside of God. And I have limped from table to table, from silence to silence, from song to song, seeking my name and hearing my new name.

But we do have to go home, although it is hard to figure out where home is. It is hard to go back because home is not what it was when we left. Even if we have been gone but a week on a pilgrimage to Chautauqua, home is not what it was. Everyone there has been pursuing the "daily-ness" of their lives—sometimes drudgery, sometimes fear. They have all been touched and changed by the week that has passed. Home is not what it used to be, but then, neither are we. We are different, too, for every pilgrimage we take changes us; and the strangers we meet bless us; and the songs that we learn to sing, the people at home have not yet heard. It is hard to go home.

It is hard to go home because on the pilgrimage of faith we find another piece of truth about life, another piece of truth that we might not have seen when we were living in the familiarity of that space, before we left to discover the deeper truth in which God continues to reveals God's self.

Annie Dillard, one of my companions on this journey, helped me see what I was discovering on the road. In her book *Pilgrim at Tinker Creek*, she observes that in nature, only the newborns in this world are whole. She says that as adults, we are expected to be and necessarily are somewhat nibbled. Everything that lives is sliced and scarred. The butterflies have their wings notched. Grasshoppers have their legs broken off. Sharks are scarred, and there are worms in their hearts.[1]

Because our eyes have had the scales burned from them, and our ears have had the cotton taken out, we have seen and heard the truth of this life. We have come to know that it is the nature of existence to be nibbled and have come to believe that just maybe it is not a deterrent to life, but it is indeed the very character of life.

When I read Annie Dillard's description, I was moved back to the place that is the center of my own life, back to my own home. As a member of the Christian Church (Disciples of Christ), the center of our life together is the Lord's table. It is a table on which we place broken bread and a cup of wine to remind us that, at core of our existence, life is broken and poured out. And when I read that all living things are nibbled, I understood why that place at that table is my home. It is the one place to which I go each week where I am reminded of what home is.

Home is where I can take my nibbled, broken, and fractured self and participate in a banquet that has been set by a broken and wounded God. Home is where I meet the Creator and the One who defines me. The table is where I not only meet God in that broken bread and that cup, but where I meet God in the broken lives of all of those who have dared to break their lives and give them to me.

Maybe this is really what home is all about: going back to the place where we have always been and finding in that brokenness a glimpse of God. But it is more than that, for the table at which I sit each week, where bread is broken and wine is poured, is a table where I am accepted in my brokenness, where I am forgiven for not being whole, and where I learn to forgive others for not being whole. It is a table of grace. And in this pilgrimage toward the Divine, one of the critical discoveries is that we are forgiven.

I have a friend whose father died, and he's had a hard time with the death. For two years he has struggled to determine why it is that he has wrestled with his father's ghosts. And finally he said to me one day, "I now know why I can't move on in my life. I have not forgiven my father for not being what I wanted him to be."

The spiritual journey of grace is the one where we learn to forgive the past for not being what we wanted it to be, and to forgive the present for not being what we need it to be, and to forgive our own psyche for not giving us all the strength that we think we have to have, and indeed it is forgiving the future for it will never be all that we want it to be. To be able to live into tomorrow is to be able to forgive life for not being what we want. The journey toward home is one where we have discovered that life is broken and nibbled, and that in order to live, we must forgive.

But there is another thing that is central to an understanding of going home. Jesus met with his disciples at night, when he was most alone. The night when he was preparing to leave them, he sat with them, and he broke the bread, and he gave it to them, and he said, "This is me, broken." He gave them a cup and said, "This is me, poured out, life poured out."

The sanctity of life is experienced when broken human beings dare to give their brokenness to each other. The only way you can give life is for it to be broken. You cannot give anything whole. Every day is the breaking of your life into one more piece. The only way you can give your life is to break it minute by minute, hour by hour, day by day, and then to give it in community to somebody else. That is what a sacred place is. It is where people have been willing to take their broken lives, and in love and courage, give them to someone else.

It is not easy to give our broken lives because many people do not want them. One of the things I have discovered on this particular journey of my life is that there are a lot of churches who do not want our broken lives. I cannot tell you how many times I have gone to church, and what they want is my wholeness. What they want is the strength of my life. They want my courage. They want my wealth. They want my power. They want my song.

But friends, when you go to worship and you do not have a song, and when you are so broken that there is no voice left to sing, and when the words you once spoke are empty and hollow and scattered at your feet, you still have something to give. The communities of faith that learn how to receive our tears are the ones who will receive our laughter and our joy. The friends that we know, the friends who sustain us are not simply the ones with whom we rejoice in our lives, but they are the ones who receive our pain, our brokenness, our tears. We give our lives, as they are; and in giving our lives, we discover God.

The reluctant pilgrim is one who moves from home to home, through the wrestling with divine strangers and friends, in the struggle with memory and emptiness, and then goes home limping. And home is where we can give a wounded and limping self to others. It is where they will receive it even if they do not understand it, and even if it makes them uncomfortable. Home is where we sit at table with other nibbled people.

Susan Ford Wiltshire records the powerful story of her brother dying of AIDS. In the book she reflects on living with brokenness. Her heart was shattered. She says:

My image is a homely one. I think of a biscuit, hot from the oven on Sunday mornings, how we break it open to butter it on both halves. The more surface space, the more honey it will hold.

The jagged edges along the break of one's heart expose more surfaces to pain. They also offer more surfaces to connect with the pain of others. A heart scored by grief embraced is a heart prepared to know and hold the grief of others. Like recognizes like.[2]

Welcome home, where hearts are broken and hold more honey. Welcome to the table of grace where a burned and frightened Moses can sit, where a grieving and witnessing Mary Magdalene can sit, where a Jacob with his wounded hip can sit on his donut ring, where an Elijah stares a silent stare into sacred hope, and where Mary hums her Hannah song. Welcome to where a broken and wounded Jesus offers himself as a glimpse of dawn.

12

Ending Relationships
and Sermons

When I began preaching, I had two major problems—
beginning the sermon and ending the sermon. I began to solve
the first problem when I read Fred Craddock's book *As One
without Authority*. Dr. Craddock developed the concept that
effective preaching assumes that the preacher does not have the
authority to tell the listener what to do or what to believe. In our
culture, therefore, it is best if the preacher develops inductive
sermons. These are sermons that begin with the particular and
move to the general. They begin with a particular question or
a particular event. The event evokes a journey of discoveries.[1]
I found that I could begin a sermon with stories about events
that provoked questions and then guide the listener through a
journey of discovery.

But I still had trouble ending sermons. How do we know
when we have taken the listener through enough of a journey?
I was still operating on the assumption that the purpose of
preaching was to give people enough insight or understanding
that they would come to agree with me about what is right
and good and would change their life accordingly. That being
the case, I did not have much help in determining when I had
been on a journey long enough. For years when I would ask
my family how my sermon went, they would gently say, "It

was good. But you could have ended about three paragraphs earlier, and it would have been better."

My anxiety drove me to overwork and to speak too much. Because I wanted people to understand me and believe what I was saying, I would work hard in being thorough with my argument and my evidence. This was so much a part of me that I am sure that I pushed people away with my intensity.

But when I now think of preaching as the art of facilitating healing relationships, I now imagine the ending of a sermon differently. My job in the sermon is not to convince people that they should believe me and motivate them to embrace my way with the actions of their life. My job is to invite people into a relationship with one or more characters. It is to give enough information about the persons I am introducing them to that they will pursue their own relationship in their own time. I am to give them enough to tease them toward more discovery.

My job as a preacher is not to say all there is nor to convince the listener that she should like the other or pursue a relationship with them. My job is to say enough to each party in the relationship that they glimpse the possibility for enrichment if they deepen their relationship. It is time for the sermon to end when I have shared some things that the parties might have in common and some differences that might be important. I do not need to milk all possible meaning for them. I need to walk with them on their journey of discovery and know that it is the journey that is the meaning, not some conclusion or final solution. I have to trust that the meaning of the relationship will be known in its own time. It is not up to me to define.

This is because endings, like beginnings and developments of sermons, are theological experiences. What we believe about God shapes what we seek to do in a sermon. What we believe about God's actions in the world shape the sermon and how the sermon ends.

I believe God is the creative reality that makes all things new. God takes the combination of energies that create what is and reshapes them into new creatures. God is that which reconfigures the particles of energy that combine to create lives that move toward a more just and loving way of being in relationship. To be alive is to be in the constant process of becoming.

Because I believe that God is creating all things new and that God is the energy of life that moves toward more just and loving relationships, I believe the ending of a sermon must leave room for that new creation to emerge in the heart and life of the listener. For this to occur, the sermon must end in the hands of mystery. For whatever we can say about God as a result of the insights from creation and the revelations through the biblical stories, God is vast mystery. And it is in that mystery that new life is possible.

The X factor helps us see how mystery holds all that we know and embodies the relationships that we have. Growing and being transformed are the result of being introduced to more of the strangers that live outside the small circle around the middle of the X. Strangers stretch our inner circle and help us be more than we know ourselves to be. As we grow, we become more familiar with the fullness of creation as it is revealed in the past, in the present, in the soul, and in the future. But as the X extends further out from the center, the mystery becomes larger. The more we know, the more we do not know. The relationships beyond the center are infinite. They are as infinite as the universe that expands beyond our globe. Those unknown relationships that are still to be discovered will be help in the empty space of mystery. As a person of faith, I believe that mystery is God.

So for a sermon to end as relationships end, there is still far more to be known than what we know. There is still more creation emerging than we have yet experienced.

But we do not end simply lost in empty mystery. We have seen clues that are now part of our constellation of relationships. The clues about how God is at work in the world of individuals and communities come to us from the biblical stories. Our relationship with the biblical characters gives us hints as to how the divine works and what healing and reconciliation might look like. But these are clues, and there are many more clues for us to discover.

I recently experimented with the concept of preaching as ending in mystery. I was asked to preach at Texas Christian University's Ministers' Week a few years ago. Struck by what we don't know and how much we can gain from our deepening relationship with biblical characters, I decided to take one story about one person and preach three different sermons on it. I selected Luke's account of the conversion of the Apostle Paul. (Acts 9:1–19). Sermons on this familiar passage have often given the preacher a chance to talk about the power of God to change people. The preacher is delighted that God can do this and invites the listener to share the delight.

But my reading of the text has led me to see more. In three sermons (one each day) I tried to discover some of the more troublesome parts of Paul's experience. I wanted to listen to and identify with the consequences of this encounter in his life. In the first sermon ("Stunned Still") I explored how God's presence stunned Paul and slowed him down to notice truths about himself. God's sudden intervention in our routine often stops us in our tracks—forcing us to face dimensions of ourselves that we would just as soon ignore. The second sermon on the same text ("Scrambled Senses") explored the way Paul became disoriented and was unable to rely on the primary sense of sight—but how when he could not see, he was forced to listen. It observed that God's coming among us often confuses what we have relied on and drives us to discover other ways of knowing truth. The third sermon ("Saving Strangers") examined this same text with an eye toward how Paul's silence and loss of sight opened him up to the gift of strangers. I sought to explore how we are often driven into the arms of strangers when God's terrifying presence forces us to become disoriented and confused.

In the exploration of this one report on Paul's experience, I discovered that there was much more we can know about the life of faith when we explore more depth of Paul's experience than we may have first glimpsed. If we end each sermon with discoveries that leave open more mystery, we will enhance the possibility for more enriching relationships.

By ending the sermon in mystery, we leave the listener with the awareness that there are clues for living, but that no sermon, no relationship, answers all our needs in life. We help them see that life is messy and cannot be summed up in predictable conclusions. We leave them hungering for more. We leave them open to the desire to discover more about the persons we have introduced them to in the sermon. We leave them with the mystery of continuing companionship.

And when we end a sermon in mystery, we leave the listener with the awareness that we know their lives are their own. One of the things that angers me as a listener to sermons is getting a sense from the preacher that he knows all there is to know about me and the person from the text he is introducing. When he ends a sermon with the conclusion neatly tied up, he is implying that there is no possibility that my relationship with the people in the sermon might lead me in a different direction. My uniqueness is denied, and I become just another person like everyone else. When you deny my uniqueness, you deny me the privilege of developing my own life of faith.

One danger of neat conclusions is that it sets the listener up for disillusionment. When we preach as if the faith means only one thing and that we must believe it as presented, the listener may do fine as long as life does not present other issues that cannot be neatly summed up the way we have been told it is.

In the 2005 movie *An Unfinished Life*,[2] Einer lived a solitary life in the big sky country of Wyoming. He lived a daily routine of bitterness as he grieved the death of his son and cared for Mitch, an old ranch hand bedridden for a year after being mauled by a bear. Einer was locked into his life—visiting his son's grave every day. Life was finished.

Finished, that is, until his late son's wife, Jean, showed up with her daughter, Griff, looking for a place to live. Einer believed that Jean was responsible for his son's death. He had been alienated from her, not knowing of his granddaughter's existence. In his struggle to discover how to live with this new situation, Einer discovered that his life was not over. He discovered that he could love—that his heart that had become stone-cold with the death of his son, could be thawed out by the persistent presence of a little girl. He discovered that even when he thought it was all over, life is unfinished. There is some more life even when we believe there is not.

When we begin sermons with an eye to introducing strangers to each other and we develop a sermon to facilitate the deepening of a relationship, we end a sermon the way we would end relationships. We end them wrapped in mystery.

We leave the listeners room to wander with the divine they have encountered in the sermon and in that wandering, to be transformed.

So if we do not end sermons by wrapping them up in neat, clean conclusions, what do we need to pay attention to? I was pondering this as I observed an "ending" that gave me some clues.

I was waiting outside my daughter's church while she was finishing up her Sunday morning responsibilities. The youth group was leaving on a mission trip, and the bus had arrived. The youth were gathered with duffle bags and backpacks, excited chatter filling the air. Parents milled around uncertain what to do. As the time of departure came, I saw Julia hug her two sons as they got on the bus. She hugged them hard, looked them in the face, and said something to them. She kissed them and let them go.

I sat and wondered about this departure. What was going on as Julia said good-bye? What did it feel like to Julia? I imagined that there was sadness over the anticipation of her boys not being at home and probably worry about their safety. There was some relief that they had gotten everything together and made it to the bus on time. There was fear for life among strangers. There was gratitude for the adult sponsors who were taking a week to travel with the kids. There was anticipation of freedom to be alone without the boys. There was an almost immediate "missing" of the presence, and then a hope for their return. I suspect as the bus pulled away, Julia wished she had said more to her boys about taking care of themselves.

In this brief scene, I came across several things that are part of endings that are not permanent. These can give us clues as to how to end relationships in sermons.

Anxiety

When a relationship is coming to an end, some people become anxious. Even if the separation is for a brief time, these people want to hang on. Young children go through an anxious time when they are separating from their mothers. It is sometimes hard for them to believe that the separation is not permanent and that their mothers will return.

When you have facilitated a relationship with someone within a sermon, listeners might feel some anxiety when the sermon is coming to an end. If they have found your introduction and deepening to be interesting and tantalizing, they may be anxious when you start to wrap it up.

People who are anxious may want fast and decisive endings. I know a man who hated saying good-bye. When his kids and grandkids began their journeys back to their own homes, he would disappear into the house. His wife would stand and wave and watch until the car was out of sight, but he just disappeared.

What can the preacher do to reduce the anxiety of endings?

The preacher's best strategy is to not be anxious herself. When we who are in the business of facilitating the relationship can communicate that the ending is not permanent, we can help the listener be less anxious. When we can leave things unfinished and room for mystery and not be anxious about that, the listener can deal with their own anxiety better. The preacher can communicate her minimal anxiety by alluding to the questions that are still to be explored as we anticipate gathering on other occasions to go deeper in our discoveries. She can exhibit her confidence that life will be fine "till we meet again."

Sadness

When I listen to sermons by Barbara Brown Taylor or Fred Craddock I have a tinge of sadness when they are over as they are so effective in their connecting me with the people within the four quadrants of my life. The relationship has been so rich and so enjoyable that I hate to end it.

But we can end sermons in such a way that the characters we meet do not have to leave us when the sermon is over. Barbara Brown Taylor does a masterful job of this in her sermon, "The One to Watch."[3] She introduces us to the widow who put two coins in the treasury of the temple. She observes that Jesus is the one who notices the woman in the midst of all the rich, intelligent, educated, and important people present. Jesus noticed a woman who had become faceless when she became a widow and pointed her out to his disciples. He did not criticize the others and their gifts, but simply pointed out how this woman gave all she had. Taylor observes that he probably notices the woman because he saw himself in her—one who would give up all he had.

After introducing us to the widow and helping us identify with her unimportance in the social setting, Dr. Brown Taylor concludes this way:

> I keep thinking I see her as I drive around town. It would sound better if I told you that I have been looking for her, but that is not really true. She is not one of the people I look for; she is more like one of the people I try not to see, but now that Jesus has pointed her out to me she is harder and harder to miss. The problem is, I am never positive it is her. Only she knows that for sure, but there are certain clues I am willing to share with you.
>
> She is not a main character, for one thing. While her appearance was memorable, they are all cameos; if you have no peripheral vision, you may miss her altogether. Sometimes she is a he, sometimes she is a child, and sometimes she is even a scribe. Now you see her, now you don't. So if you want to spot her you have to watch, really watch, because you never know where she will turn up next.
>
> The second clue is that she is usually giving something away: her time, her heart, her living, her life. The general rule is that you cannot see how much it costs her, but it is almost always more than you think
>
> The third clue is that what she is doing rarely makes sense by any ordinary human standard. It is as if she gets her orders from some other planet, where superior beings know things we do not yet know—such as how to let go of the little that you have in order to receive the more you do not, or how to trust what you cannot see more than you trust what you can.
>
> That is as far as I have gotten with clues, but you can probably come up with some more of your own. Here is what you do. You sit down somewhere where you can get a good look at whatever is going on, and

you pay special attention to what is happening out on the edges of your vision, where people are sometimes hard to see. Then you crunch your eyes just slightly and ask yourself: "Where is Christ in this picture?"[4]

Notice how this ending works to open the imagination to the empty spaces that will follow the sermon and continue the relationships begun in the sermon. We are given clues as to what to look for and some direction on how to position ourselves to look. We are then guided to see in the "unnoticed" other the possibility that Christ is present. The relationship with the widow, and through her our relationship with Christ, can continue. Sadness can be softened when we know that the presence of the ones we got to know might continue in another quadrant of our memory.

Fear

When Julia left her sons and they got on the bus, I sensed some fear in her eyes. This may be my own memories coming into consciousness through the presence of this mother saying good-bye. When we send our children off to a part of the world with which we are not very familiar, we worry about their safety.

When a sermon ends and we have developed a relationship with someone in the sermon, there may be some fear attached to the ending of the sermon. Earlier I introduced you to a friend of mine who worked on her doctoral dissertation for several years and then sank into major depression after she finished it. What I failed to do was realize that one of my listeners had experienced a similar situation and could identify with my friend. It frightened her. So when I finished the sermon, I was invited to continue the conversation so that the listener had some sense that the person in the sermon was now OK. This gave her hope that she would be OK too. In looking back on this experience, I could have added one more sentence to the sermon, such as, "She has since discovered her way again, but it was frightening for her as it happened." Had I included that in the sermon, the listener who shared the experience might have received a word of hope in the sermon.

Sermons that end the way relationships end must acknowledge that there might still be some fear without having clear and predictable conclusions. But it is that fear that contributes to our leaning forward to know and discover more.

Regret

Regret is often an emotion that accompanies the ending of a relationship. Regardless of the positive and fulfilling dimensions of a relationship, when it ends, the people involved often feel regret that more was not experienced. When a relationship ends, people are often sorry that they did not commit more time or share more experiences together.

As I think of my dad's death over ten years ago, I still have regrets. We had a good relationship and we were blessed with more opportunities for shared life than many. But still there are stories I did not hear and did not ask about. I regret that I did not ask him about the sounds and smells of the trains as he rode boxcars across the West to find work. I regret that I did not hear more stories about his years as a young man at John Brown University in Siloam Springs, Arkansas. I do not know of any relationship that does not have regrets and wishes for more.

But these can be good things for living in the future. As we remember what we did not do or know with persons with whom our relationships have ended, we can develop our present relationships more fully. We can ask more questions. We can make more time to share our lives. We can give more of our emotional energy to the relationships we have now.

Regrets at the end of a sermon can have both damaging and positive results. If a person has hopes and expectations for a sermon that are unrealistic and those expectations are not met, they can become angry and take it out on the preacher. If the preacher makes people believe that her sermon on the suffering of innocent people will answer all questions to their satisfaction, they may be very angry when they discover that there are no good answers. It is important in the beginning of sermons to clarify what you hope to do and what you cannot accomplish in this sermon. To help reduce the impact of the regret, begin a sermon by saying what you are not going to do along with what you hope can happen.

But there are some positive dimensions of regret at the end of a sermon. If a person feels like the sermon simply got them interested in some character in the Bible but did not really fulfill the desire to know more, regret can help motivate further action on their part. Regret can turn to appreciation as the listener moves from the pew to the computer to explore further some story mentioned from the morning news. The listener has the privilege of sharing in the discovery, and the sermon functions to stimulate curiosity that keeps the listener interested and deepening their relationship with the person to whom they were introduced in the sermon.

Companionship

Sermons that facilitate healing relationships do not end by tying up the ideas in a neat and complete package. They end with room for the imagination to take the relationship into that unknown future and explore more possibilities. They end with unresolved questions the way most of our encounters end.

People need to get wrapped up in a narrative to have some satisfaction in the encounter. While we will never know all the mystery of the other nor will we have answers to all our questions in life, it is important when the relationship facilitated in the sermon ends that the listener feel the encounter has been worth their time. The best that we can probably do is to help the person experience others in the sermon so when they leave they will know that they are not alone. The hope is that the resolution will be the discovery that life is a shared journey. In what we discover in our relationship with creation and the creatures of this earth, we will experience the presence of the divine creator.

My friend Dick preached a sermon on Jonathan's love for David. He spoke of brothers who care for each other and how important it is that we not live life alone. After the service, a woman whom Dick did not know shook his hand. With tears rimming her eyes, she looked Dick in the eye and said, "I came to the right church this morning. I think God led me here. I have a son named Jonathan, and I just said good-bye to him yesterday as he was shipped out to Iraq." Dick introduced Jonathan and

David's love to the congregation. This woman left knowing that she and her son, though separated, were not alone.

This is the intent of my sermon on Jacob's wrestling ("The Familiar Strangers") when I describe the pilgrimage of the soul in the dark with "those characters of our own soul whom we do not know." At the conclusion of the sermon, I try to help the listener leave feeling connected with Jacob and people like him who have been touched by the divine and changed. Leaving a sermon without all the answers but with companions for the journey into the future gives persons a sense of satisfaction in having been present for the sermon.

Hope

> For in hope we are saved. Now hope that is seen is not hope. For who hopes for what is seen? But if we hope for what we do not see, we wait for it with patience. (Rom. 8:24)

Hope is the capacity to take our memories, our contemporary experiences, and our soulful life and imagine them into an unknown future. Hope is the holding space for the lives we are moving toward. Hope is the empty space in which new creation takes place. Without hope, without the empty future whispering us forward into the unknown, relationships are not alive. They do not give us life.

When relationships end, they do not end. They simply morph into new relationships. When someone's partner dies, the relationship as it was known and experienced has ended. But the partner continues to live in the memory and as that memory infiltrates our world and comes alive in our future.

Mike lost his wife to cancer, but she continued to live in his memory. He had locations of memorial such as the lake on which he had scattered her ashes. By going to those places of memory, she lived on with him and informed how he made decisions. When he would think about how to dress his little girl, he remembered his wife and what she wanted for her.

This is the way relationships continue to live after a sermon has ended. In the space called hope, the encounter between the listener and the people introduced to the listener in the sermon continues. It changes as the memory of the encounter is integrated into the listener's life. But when one has been effective in facilitating the relationship, the listener is blessed with a continuing presence of the person met in the sermon.

I conclude my sermon "Sounds of Silence" with the effort to create in the listener a longing for the empty spaces in which new life can emerge. Describing the barren and wounded mountain scenes at St. Helen, I tried to evoke an experience of surprise for listeners—as I myself had experienced surprise at finding the flowers and new life sprouting out of stumps and ash. The ending of a sermon that facilitates healing relationships leaves much empty space for the relationship to bloom into what is possible. It does not force but trusts that with patience the relationship will develop and God will use it to bring healing to the listener.

Promise

When we preach regularly to the same congregation, we always live with the promise that the relationships with God and God's people will be steadfast. The nature of a faith community is to reflect the steadfast presence of the divine. Our world is a celebrity world—people are loved for a day, and then the culture seeks out someone else to worship when celebrities fail to live up to expectations. The nature of the church is to counter that capricious faith by being faithful and continuing to show up.

The preacher ends sermons with the sense that the persons introduced will be back to deepen their relationships. This promise of faithful presence on the part of the sacred texts and their stories and on the part of the community committed to God's action in the world is the context for the ending of a sermon. Without this promise, the preacher has the pressure to make each sermon complete unto itself. That pressure and that desire to complete each sermon and tie it up with neat bows forces the preacher to reduce the content of a sermon. When sermons are reduced so they can be finished, they become more fixed and less alive and more predictable and less transforming. The listener and the participant in the community have responsibility for their own faith development and that requires that they be faithful in their participation. When that happens the ending of a sermon is not a permanent ending–it is a "see you next week" ending. It is a "talk to you later" relationship based on a commitment on the part of each to mutual care and concern.

To end a sermon gracefully is to help people attend to their feelings, helping them develop trust that the relationship will continue. Assert confidence in their ability to make discoveries within themselves. Leave them with the hunger that provokes their own search for deeper relationships. You are not their savior. Their saving relationships are those you help facilitate by your preaching.

Creating an Oral Cathedral

It was time to go to worship. The sun bore down with unusual intensity in western New York. The thousands were gathering for Sunday worship. Barbara Brown Taylor was the preacher of the week at the Chautauqua Institution.

My friends and I took our usual position, some distance from the pulpit. As a recently "liberated" pulpit person, I did not want to be too close. My few experiences of sitting in the pew at worship services since my wife of thirty years died of cancer had taught me that. Preachers seemed to overwhelm a wounded and vulnerable listener, so it is always good to keep your distance if you do not want your boundaries violated.

But that morning in the steamy heat, we sat and listened. And when we went to worship the next morning, we moved a little closer. The third morning, we were in the second row. We leaned into every word, allowing them to take up residence in our soul. We heard the preacher as she spun stories of grace. My soul did not recoil in fear.

As one who had weekly broken the word with parishioners for over thirty years, I was intrigued. "What was it about this preaching that drew us closer? Why were we not driven back against our seats?"

I decided, since I was heading to a seminary to teach preaching, I should ask Barbara to help me understand what shapes her preaching. Over coffee I asked her, "What do you think makes your preaching effective?" In good Socratic style she said, "What do *you* think makes it effective?" (As a seminary professor I have discovered that a question in response to a question is always better than saying, "I don't know.")

I had not expected her question. So after sipping coffee and stalling with "hmmms" and "ughs," I finally said, "I don't know, but you seem to create safe space into which a listener can move. It's almost like you create a space for the spirit of the listener to move toward your words, and in that encounter, Holy Spirit creates community." I do not know what all was said after that, but her answer, (or was it my answer?) has haunted me since that day. I had been preaching for over thirty years, and I had read and listened to preachers and teachers of preachers. And I had never quite seen preaching that way. She created a sanctuary where the listener was safe to encounter a community-making spirit.

As I began to teach preaching, I helped students think about how to create a sanctuary with words—how to create a safe space into which the listener might move so that she can imagine and "word their way" into some new way of living. Later I was visiting the National Cathedral in Washington, DC and I realized that I had been trying to help students learn to build an oral cathedral in which all people might gather to explore the grand mystery of the divine. I tried to help them create space within that mystery to know themselves and their world in a new way.

Preaching is creating space in which persons find words to know who they are and how they can live faithfully. Some listeners are learning it for the first time. Others have lost their ability to voice their own story and need to learn new words. We are constantly in process of rewording our lives. We redefine ourselves with different stories. Words that had once defined me—"pastor," "preacher," "husband"—had become devoid of meaning. I had to find words that resonate more with my current experience. In the empty spaces "between" known and unknown, familiar and unfamiliar, we huddle in fear and confusion hoping for a sanctuary for our fragile and stuttering voice to whisper new possibilities.

When Barbara spoke, she created an oral cathedral where I could go and whisper my own words. And in that space, I discovered that a cloud of witnesses to the same journey surrounded me as I was traveling. My lonely, ragged, scared, frightened and coarse voice of grief was joined by the anguish and ecstasy of the voices of those who lived in the walls of memory. In the company of the saints, I found courage to speak truth about my own life. The way Barbara spoke and the words she used gave my voices permission to be heard. It was almost a resurrection of the dead voices of my soul.

How does one know if one is in an oral cathedral? How do we preach to create such a sanctuary space?

Cathedrals

A cathedral is entered through gigantic doors. They are far taller and wider than one person would need to enter. They are doors created with size, welcoming *all* who come to enter. Their size is invitational, not demanding. One has a choice—to enter and be swallowed by shadowed mystery or turn and retreat.

Through these vast doors, a *whole* community—stranger and friend, alien and enemy—gathers in the presence of a mystery grand beyond each and all. A cathedral is a space where light and shadow wrestle on the floor, where knowing and unknowing play tag among the pews. A cathedral is not a space where color and light are fixed and unchanging. It is a place where light pierces color and creates changing images in the air. Colors tumble over each other in a kaleidoscopic delight.

Cathedrals create a space in which the soul's cacophonous voices can be drawn out into a safe space. They create stimuli to seduce the words from the depth of the repressed and controlled world in which many live and encourage them to center around a mysterious reality of grace and mercy. Cathedrals create communities whose character is formed by the space.

A cathedral is a space where words are bathed in beauty, and language is laced with incense. It is a place where music reaches beyond the heights and below the depths. It houses fire that flickers, casting its heat to warm cold hearts and its light to illumine the frightening dark.

A cathedral is also a place where time has an eternal quality. It is a place where the immediacy of urgent time is stretched into the expanse of timeless time. It is a place where time reaches back through the ages in memory and stares ahead into eternal wondering. A cathedral is a place where there is time to wander through the stained-glass stories, allowing ourselves to be stained by their humanity and divinity. It is a place where ordinary people seem to dance from the windows with a quality of illuminating saint-like life.

How does preaching create an oral sanctuary? How do we speak so that there is a sanctuary space in which the listeners might move without fear? How do we speak to create space between the tongue and the ear so that the spirit might have room to embrace both?

Oral Cathedral

Central to creating an oral cathedral is respect for boundaries. If the speaker has the need to fill the room with his own presence, there is no room for others. A speaker who knows her own boundary does not intrude on the space of others. Her presence will allow room for the soul of another to be present. The architecture of the sermon represents itself for what *it* is, not intruding into the sacred space of another and demanding that the listeners be something that they are not.

I remember being in a large convention at which a person was preaching. I was so overwhelmed by the way she filled the room that I had to sit under the bleachers at the back of the convention hall. There was no space for me. When a preacher is driven to change others, she may be tempted to push into the space of others. But if she understands her role as one who bears witness to understandings that have overtaken her, she can make them an offering to the listener without needing the listener to affirm, agree, or accommodate. A preacher centered in her own soul can allow the fire to burn deeply and furiously and keep it contained so that it warms the heart of the other, rather than burning the other with blistering pain.

A person who bears witness to that which has overtaken him is able to speak with humility. When a preacher knows that he is speaking out of a power that he cannot control and manipulate, he can then speak with the humility of one who knows some things but whose knowing is encompassed in an expansive universe of mystery. If he speaks of this glimpse of knowing and helps the listener realize that there is much to be learned, the listener can lean into that space and make her offering, broken and incomplete, to the community of discovery. The preacher becomes a tour guide who knows that the vast power and history of the cathedral's memory quiets the soul's arrogant assumptions. When we speak with humility, people trust the truth they hear from us. When we speak in ways that presume to know more than any human can know, the listener intuitively rejects it because they know that it could not be true.

One of the most effective ways of communicating humility is by telling particular and concrete stories. We tell a story with all its particularity and humanity and persons can see themselves in it. We can then wonder about what the story might mean, musing about possible interpretations. These musings, grounded in reality of creaturely existence, have the ability to only "point to meaning," not create a comprehensive understanding for all times and places. We cannot extrapolate immortal truth from mortal stories.

The cathedral walls dance with the light filtered through the stained glass colors. The shadows and light struggle for supremacy, each winning and losing, each giving and taking. If we speak with some photographic precision that assumes fixed truth, the listener will know that it is untrue. The words of a sermon that ring true to the mystery of who is God are words that have some "maybe" and some "on-the-other hand" order to them.

We not only speak with boundaries intact, but we also speak with care. A cathedral was built over time with love and care. Sometimes it took decades to build. The tools of the craftsperson become sacred in their careful attention to detail in the stone and the glass. Oral cathedrals are sermons that reflect careful and thoughtful attention. The preacher who attends carefully to the words she is using helps the listener feel that she has respect for all words. If the preacher respects the words of the ancient texts enough to handle them with care, maybe she will handle the fragile words of my soul with care too. The preacher creates a space for my deepest words when she carefully prepares words for my ears to hear. It is almost a Pentecost space. At Pentecost, multiple voices were heard and assimilated into the hearts of the hearers. The Holy Spirit created a sense of community out of diverse languages. When the preacher respects even the words she does not understand (or especially the words she does not understand), she creates a sanctuary for my confusion to be spoken and maybe integrated into a community of unity.

A cathedral is bathed with color from sun-stained glass. A stained-glass window allows light to illumine story. A well-crafted sermon will be light refracted by story. The stained glass has representations of humans in all forms of joy and suffering. The glory and the agony of human life are represented in death and dance, resurrection and turmoil. Sermons that tell stories of real human experience create space so that real human joy and confusion might enter. Stories of strangers whom God uses to illumine divine truth help the listener to imagine the stranger next to him in the pew as a possible mediator of divine grace. Stories of God's welcome of the marginal in society help create communities of people sensitive to the injustices in our societies. Stories of confused and frightened disciples allow a chaotic soul to imagine that he too might have place among the company of discovering disciples.

A delight of cathedrals is that they are so large that they create a sense of wonder and space to wander in that wonder. When one wanders into the National Cathedral in Washington, DC, one gets a sense that one could spend the whole day, or a week, and never fully know the space. It is rich with layers of meaning, with images of ancient worlds and expansive future worlds. Every image and sound sends the mind wandering among the wonders of existence. An oral cathedral is one in which there is space and size. There is room to wander around. It is cohesive enough that people know they are in a space whose integrating core is divine mystery, but it is roomy enough that a listener can wander down aisles and stare at unimagined insight. If a sermon is so tight that it leaves no room for the imagination to search its own mysteries, the soul has trouble feeling safe to come out with its own voices.

In a cathedral, time is also different. It seems to have an eternal, ethereal quality. Refracted through patterned light and resting in the arms of ancient aesthetics, time seems to slow down. One gets a sense that maybe all the joys in life are not reserved for those who race through it. One gets a sense that the temporal might not be all there is to time. When a preacher creates an oral cathedral, she opens the heart of the listener to the aesthetic grace of ancient wisdom. She does this by attention to the beauty of the language. Poetry slows the racing heart and allows language to take its time. Attention to the way words feel on the tongue and sound to the ear helps the preacher speak with a sense of timelessness. Attention to meter and alliteration can help the aesthetics of the spoken word please the ear's palate.

When the preacher creates an oral cathedral, he creates a space in which the listener might glimpse truth and worship it with voice and song, with self and soul. On my refrigerator is a quote—it has been there for twenty years. I do not know where it came from, but it says, "Truth, like love and sleep, resists an approach too intense." Much preaching seems too intense. It seems to create a sense of panic and urgency, pushing many people away. It partakes of the frenetic culture that seems to assume that the more we do and the more we get the better life will be.

Preaching that creates a sanctuary space is countercultural. It is more about creating a holding space in which life might be explored and practiced than propelling us into more activity, wearing down an already weary soul. People often ask for a sermon to be relevant. But, within a cathedral, the soul opens up to the holy irrelevance. The soul opens up to the possibility that beauty may be one of the most relevant realities for the soul's life. One considers the possibility that relevance might visit through the life of strangers who seem to have nothing to do with our needs and desires.

It has been several years now since that coffee with Barbara Brown Taylor sent my mind searching. The coffee is gone. The days have evaporated. But Barbara helped me discover ways to speak that create a cathedral space for others to experience the holy. The encounter with the holy stained my soul and opened me to new places in my own thought. Because there was a space for me to whisper and hear the echo of that whisper through the canyons of sacred memory, I have been able to speak again. I can now speak confidently that there are plenty of hollow spaces between my words. If there are enough of those spaces, listeners might hear holy silence; and in that silence, speak their own life into existence.

NOTES

Chapter 1: Leaving Home

[1]My mother died during the writing of this book, which is dedicated to her memory.

[2]*Shirley Valentine,* DVD, directed by Lewis Gilbert (1989, Burbank, CA: Paramount, 2007).

[3]Annie Dillard, *Pilgrim at Tinker Creek* (New York: Harper Perennial, 1974), 7.

Chapter 2: Where Pulpit and Life Meet

[1]Dan P. Moseley, "Preaching: Creating an Oral Cathedral," *The Living Pulpit* 15:1 (January-March 2006): 16–19.

Chapter 4: How Relationships Heal and Transform

[1]Fred B. Craddock, *As One without Authority* (St. Louis: Chalice Press, 2001), 131–32.

Chapter 6: The Contexts for Preaching Healing

[1]Jennifer Michael Hecht, *Doubt: A History* (San Francisco: Harpers, 2003).

[2]Richard Hamm, *Recreating the Church: Leadership for the Postmodern Age* (St. Louis: Chalice Press, 2007).

[3]Margaret J. Wheatley, *Leadership and the New Science: Learning about Organization from an Orderly Universe* (San Francisco: Berrett-Koehler, 1992).

[4]Ibid., 6.

[5]Ibid., 7.

[6]Ibid., 10.

[7]Zygmunt Bauman, *Liquid Modernity* (Cambridge, U.K.: Blackwell, 2000).

[8]Ibid., 13–14.

[9]William Bridges, *Transitions: Making Sense of Life's Changes* (Cambridge, Mass.: Da Capo Press, 2004).

[10]For an extensive exploration of the discoveries that one might make as they process the loss that results from change, see my book *Living with Loss* (Nashville: Xyzzy Press, 2007).

[11]Ibid., 45.

[12]Belden C. Lane, *The Solace of Fierce Landscapes: Exploring Desert and Mountain Spirituality* (Oxford: Oxford University Press, 1998).

[13]Aidan Kavanagh, *On Liturgical Theology* (New York: Pueblo Publishing, 1984).

[14]Ibid.

Chapter 7: Sounds of Silence

[1]Milan Kundera, *Immortality* (New York: Harper Perennial, 1991).

[2]Ibid., 223.

[3]Tim Brooks, "Dirt Roads: An Essay in Praise of Inconvenience," *US Airways Attaché Magazine* (May 2000), 72.

[4]Annie Dillard, *Pilgrim at Tinker Creek* (New York: Harper Perennial, 1974).

[5]Ibid., 163–64.

Chapter 8: Introducing People in the Beginning
of the Sermon

[1]Daniel Moseley, *Living with Loss* (Nashville: Xyzzy Press, 2007).

Chapter 9: Sacred Memory

[1]Phil Cousineau, *The Art of Pilgrimage: The Seeker's Guide to Making Travel Sacred* (Berkley: Conari Press, 1998), 111.

[2]Gerald L. Sittser, *A Grace Disguised: How the Souls Grows Through Loss* (Grand Rapids, Mich: Zondervan, 1995).

[3]Belden C. Lane, *The Solace of Fierce Landscapes: Exploring Desert and Mountain Spirituality* (Oxford: Oxford University Press, 1998).

[4]James Weldon Johnson, "Lift Every Voice and Sing," *Chalice Hymnal* (St. Louis: Chalice Press, 1995), no. 631.

Chapter 10: Deepening Relationships in the Body
of the Sermon

[1]*The Story of the Weeping Camel*, DVD-Video, directed by Luigi Falorni (New York: New Line Home Video, 2003).

[2]Thomas E. Boomershine, *Story Journey: An Invitation to the Gospel as Storytelling* (Nashville: Abingdon Press, 1988), 23–40.

Chapter 11: Coming Home

[1]Annie Dillard, *Pilgrim at Tinker Creek* (New York: Harper Perennial, 1974).

[2]Susan Ford Wiltshire, *Seasons of Grief and Grace: A Sister's Story of AIDS* (Nashville: Vanderbilt University Press, 1994), 88.

Chapter 12: Ending Relationships and Sermons

[1]Fred B. Craddock, *As One without Authority* (St. Louis: Chalice Press, 2001), 131–32.

[2]*An Unfinished Life*, DVD-Video, directed by Lasse Hallstrom (Miramax, 2006)

[3]Barbara Brown Taylor, *The Preaching Life* (Boston: Cowley Publications, 1993), 127–32.

[4]Ibid., 131–32.